A Young Person's Guide to Atheism

S.C. Hitchcock

Illustrations by
Leslie White

See Sharp Press • Tucson, Arizona

PUBLISHER'S NOTE: The use of a pseudonym by the author was dictated by the publisher. The author is a family man with young children who lives in a particularly religious part of Middle America. He has received anonymous death threats after writing letters to the local paper opposing the Iraq war. The publisher fears that worse might happen after publication of this book if it appeared under the author's true name.

Hitchcock, S. C.
   Disbelief 101: a young person's guide to atheism / S. C.
Hitchcock ; illus. by Leslie White -- Tucson, Ariz.: See Sharp
Press, 2009.
130 p. : ill. ; 23 cm.
Includes bibliographical references and index.

Contents: 1. The Invisible Flying Clown -- 2. Atheism as "Belief" --
3. Faith: A False Virtue -- 4. The Suicide King... Arguments for
God's Existence -- 5. Evolution and Religion -- 6. Two Columns:
Science and Faith -- 7. The Rock Star Principle... Why Are We
Here? -- 8. Does Anybody Ever Read This Thing? (The Bible,
That Is) -- 9. Feelings as "Proof" -- 10. Let the Buyer Beware --
11. The Darwinian God -- 12. Religious Indoctrination of
Children is Child Abuse.

1. Skepticism -- Juvenile literature. 2. Atheism -- Juvenile literature.
3. Critical thinking -- Juvenile literature.
                211.8

Contents

For my son—

Good luck, kid!

Introduction

*All humanity is here for one reason: to answer
the question of what the meaning of life is.*
— S.C. Hitchcock

Oh, to have found this book when I was thirteen.

I turned thirteen in 1968, by all accounts a momentous year. But never mind your Summer of Love, your Chicago convention riots, your Bobby Kennedy and Martin Luther King assassinations. For me 1968 was the year I first seriously questioned my Roman Catholic faith.

To grasp what a big deal that was, you need to understand that the twelve-year-old me took his religion very, very seriously. Looking back, I'm not altogether sure where that came from: my parents were devout, but no one's fanatics. Perhaps I fell under the influence of a round-the-bend Sunday-school nun. Or possibly it was all me, a smart kid too determined to weave all the tall tales and impossible miracles I'd been commanded to embrace into an internally consistent whole, never mind that it couldn't be done.

Whatever the source, I was one of those Catholic kids who believed it all and when called upon to paper over some doctrinal contradiction supplied my own wallpaper paste. I embraced my Catholicism with a literalist ardor more characteristic of evangelical Protestant fundamentalism. Adam and Eve (not a big deal among many Catholics even then), papal infallibility, the propriety of God's sending to hell whomever he chose (he was God, for crying in the sink), the irredeemable perversity of such vicious heretics as, oh, Lutherans and Baptists—I bought it all. Some nights I'd lay in bed, my chest bursting with pride that I'd had the fabulous luck to be born into the only religious community that had all the details right, the only club whose members held passes into heaven. Your Episcopalians, Jews, Quakers: mere kindling for the fires of hell. Only Roman Catholics would Jesus save. And I saw no injustice in that. By whatever joyous fortune, when the angels poured out their sacks of souls on a night roughly nine months prior to my birthday, my soul had shimmied down a chute at whose mouth quivered a zygote that would grow up Roman Catholic.

The point of all this was that when the thirteen-year-old me entertained his first doubts about the veracity of his faith, that was Crisis One in my world for 1968.

And this book was nowhere in sight.

Why religious believers often feel the need to
obsessively gather in large groups:
"How can I be crazy if everyone else
thinks the same thing?"
—S.C. Hitchcock

I've spoken with hundreds of now-lapsed Catholics; their paths toward apostasy tend to fall into one broad category or another. My first question concerned those pesky other religions, Christian and otherwise. Granted that all other churches were man's work, not God's, what evidence could I discern in the world that divine favor rested uniquely on the Church of Rome? Mounting horror attended my inability to find any. Lightning struck non-Catholic churches no more frequently. Catholicism seemed no less heir to the corruptions of politics and sex and money. (Of course at this juncture I knew nothing of the spectacular venality and concupiscence of the medieval popes. And the pederasty scandal was still decades ahead.) Just as I was obsessing on this, the reforms of the Second Vatican Council began to percolate into parish life. Watching rituals and practices I'd thought eternal uprooted by mere human choices, I conceded that my church was swayed by bureaucracy and politics no less than any other. With a hollowing fear I realized that if what I had just discovered were true, I could no longer . . . gulp . . . be a Catholic.

What a wonderful moment it would have been to discover this book.

One by one my doubts paraded. Deploy here the hackneyed metaphor of your choice: over years I planed my faith away. I peeled the onion of my superstitions. I opened one after another the nested Russian dolls of skepticism.

Okay, no more metaphors. The point is that on issue after issue, I realized that my former faith was bankrupt. With each new discovery I would stand frozen, terrified of what it implied. Why, if Catholicism is not obviously superior to the other denominations . . . if Christianity is not demonstrably superior to the other faiths . . . if the cosmos shows fewer signs of God than signs that there is no god ... With each new realization painful weeks or months would pass until I came to terms with whatever fearsome implication had terrified me so. One after another the anguished milestones passed. I acknowledged that I was no longer a Catholic . . . then, no longer a Christian . . . eventually, no longer a generic theist . . . at last, not a deist of any sort.

Then came (yes, literally) the morning when I woke up realizing that I was emotionally comfortable with atheism. Being part of an unplanned, undesigned, mutely unjust cosmos that no more cared for me than it recognized my existence was suddenly a proposition I was happy to accept. I was twenty-three; shucking off my childhood faith had cost me the better part of nine years, a slow-motion marathon of deliberation and misery and sporadic courage that I ran entirely alone, confiding in no one, relying on few if any outside sources.

Losing my religion was an altogether interior process, at the end of which the twenty-three-year-old me hauled ass to the downtown library (no Web yet) and looked up "atheism" in the card catalogue. Now that I was an atheist, it was time to know a little better what that meant. In a rush I found that others had preceded me down my lonely road. Profound thinkers had wrestled with the issues that had vexed me. There were atheist and humanist organizations, even freethinking books that could have handed me much of the knowledge I'd had to develop on my own. Wryly I recognized that if I'd known how to access these resources years earlier, my odyssey to unbelief might have unfolded far sooner, far less painfully.

Still, I found nothing quite like this book.

> If [a punitive Old Testament-style deity] is your god, then his
> actions or lack of action describe a petty tyrant, a
> sick bastard who shovels souls into bodies without regard
> for fairness, love, or happiness. He's a god who
> must enjoy all of the suffering in the world—otherwise
> it would not be here.
> It's a good thing he doesn't exist.
> —S.C. Hitchcock

With *Disbelief 101*, S. C. Hitchcock has given the world something achingly special: a book that addresses precisely the fears and obsessions that seize young people of rock-ribbed faith when they first begin to doubt.

You see, my experience wasn't all that unusual. Today I know more atheists and humanists and freethinkers than just about anyone else I know, and I've spent years listening to them about how most of them lost their childhood faiths. (Yes, some people grow up as atheists, but most non-religious Americans were brought up in one faith or another and had to think their way out of it.) Though each such odyssey is unique, broad patterns can be discerned. Slow, painful, jerky progress is common. Way too often, new-freethinkers regard the just-discovered genre of free-thought publications and say, "If only I'd found these books and magazines and web sites earlier—I could have saved years!"

And that's why I know *Disbelief 101* has a special contribution to make.

> *Understand this: If religions don't indoctrinate children, they will cease to exist. They can only survive by using childhood indoctrination techniques.*
> —S.C. Hitchcock

If you're a young person who used to believe it all, but now you're starting to doubt—or if you know a young person answering that description—this book may be a life-changer. I've never seen a volume that compresses into fewer words, or expresses in clearer concepts, the very things a young zealot needs to think about before beginning the personal truth quest that may culminate in unbelief.

Over the years I've discovered lots of books that made me say, "If only I'd read this book back when I first began to disbelieve." Of all these books, *Disbelief 101* does the most thorough job of distilling just the ideas, just the evidence, and just the exhortation a young doubter needs to complete the journey toward unbelief more fluently and with less pain.

Longtime (or lifelong) freethinkers may wonder at some of the things S. C. Hitchcock has chosen to include or leave out. They may think too much energy is invested in debunking sophomoric theological conceptions, too little in constructing the platform for living a life of humane values without religion. (Though in fact, S.C. offers vivid demonstrations why irreligion beats religion hands down at encouraging ethical living.)

If you are one who has never known the agony and wonder of dismantling a deeply held faith, please take the counsel of one who has. *Disbelief 101* is not a book for those who've always disbelieved. It addresses the specific terrors and confusions that come with shedding the husk of youthful certainties. Weird as this may seem to lifelong atheists, countless young apostates lose years trapped between the intellectual knowledge that God does not exist and the emotional fear of being pitched into hell for daring to think such a thing. S.C. Hitchcock gets that, maybe better than any other author I've read.

While reading *Disbelief 101*, I was envious to discover the explosive book that would best have addressed my own deepest fears and obsessions when I was a novice inquirer. Nothing could have spared the thirteen-year-old me more years, more torment, than to have somehow been able to crack open *Disbelief 101* across my lap in that tumultuous year of 1968.

I use the word *explosive* deliberately. S.C. Hitchcock's book has the potential to empower many, many, many young zealots to outgrow their childhood religions. Yet S.C. lives in Middle America. Sadly, I believe he is wise to write under a pseudonym. If this book winds up shaping as many young atheists as I expect it might—if, as it deserves, it someday joins Paine's *The Age of Reason* and the Bible itself among the books that most prolifically free young readers from their faiths—Middle America may not remain safe for its author.

I'm in my fifties now, inhabiting a different world than my 13-year-old self. I genuinely believe that before I die I may see an America that accepts atheists, agnostics, humanists, and freethinkers as readily as Catholics and Lutherans now look past one another's differences. As I've often written, I think the key to achieving this is simply to foment disbelief among the young, and to encourage every young unbeliever to be maximally visible so our true numbers will be impossible to undercount. *Disbelief 101* has the potential to be a powerful weapon in that campaign.

> *Religion relies and thrives on your fear. But don't*
> *be afraid. God doesn't exist.*
> —S.C. Hitchcock

If you know a young doubter, give her or him this book.

If you are a young doubter, keep reading. And welcome home.

—Tom Flynn

(Tom Flynn is the editor of *Free Inquiry* magazine and *The New Encyclopedia of Unbelief*.)

Acknowledgments

No one writes a book alone, and I'd like to thank a number of people who made this book possible. First and foremost, I'd like to thank my wife, who always seems to understand when I need time to write. I'd like to thank Chaz Bufe of See Sharp Press for taking a chance on this book and for his always wise editorial guidance. Tom Flynn deserves my gratitude for being an early reader, for his sage advice on all things godless, and for his fine introduction. Sharon Berger, too, gave me good advice. I'd also like to thank Ashley Grayson for his early advocacy. Finally, many other atheists and humanists were early readers, and I have come to believe that there are no people more generous of spirit than those who do not believe.

Preface

THERE IS NO GOD.

Some people find the notion that there is no god upsetting, although the idea is completely rational and sane. Perhaps they upset themselves about it because it is rational and sane. And, if those people are in charge of your life, they may be walking around the very bookstore or library in which you are reading this. If that's the case, and you only have a second to read a few sentences, then close this book, but take the first sentence with you. Keep it to yourself, but remember: There is no god.

If you're still reading, I assume that you've found a safe place to hunker down, or enlightened people are in charge of your life, or you've taken the cover off *A Purpose Driven Life* and wrapped it around this book. Whatever you've done, good for you. You've taken the first step toward freeing your mind.

In the following chapters I'll show the absurdity of all religions and their shared notion of a god or gods. It won't take much to show this. It's amazing that religion has survived as long as it has—it seems as if all it would take to make anyone an atheist is ten minutes of practical thought. All of the arguments in favor of a god can be brushed away like spider webs, and when you finish this book you'll probably be asking yourself why religion continues to exist. The answer is simple: Religion survives and is a huge force in the world because it relies on the indoctrination of children.

In short, this book is for young people whose minds have been abused by religious indoctrination. If you are a young person who was or is being forced to go to church, Sunday school, synagogue, or mosque, to pray, to seek nirvana, or a higher power—or to believe in any number of crazy things—then you've been abused mentally. If you've been taught that belief, that faith, is a good thing, you have been tricked.

You deserve better than to be tricked and indoctrinated. You deserve to be given the tools of free inquiry—the tools to make up your own mind. You deserve to be able to take ownership of your own brain without having it cluttered with nonsense. But, unfortunately, in this country and in the rest of the world, all too many children are abused by having religion thrust upon them when they are too young to protect themselves.

Religion is like smoking. Few people take up smoking in adulthood. The tobacco industry relies on the fact that young people, who are impressionable, take up the habit when they are too young to see the consequences. By the time a smoker is old enough to see the error of his or her ways, it's too late. They are addicted. Similarly, few clear-thinking adults become religious; most adults became religious when religion was forced on them at a young age. If I forced a child to smoke—which harms her body—that would be abuse. Forcing religion on a child—which harms her mind—is also abuse.

In the following chapters, I'll lay out logical arguments in as simple and enjoyable a way as possible. I will steer clear of topics like politics and law. I won't complain about stem cell research or Supreme Court decisions.

What I will show you is how to think and how to take ownership of your mind. It may not be easy—once the image of a god has been branded on your mind's eye, it's difficult not to see everything through the scar—but it is possible.

In a way, I'm very sorry to do this. There is simply no way of getting around the fact that I'll be calling some of the people who may be dearest to you, some of the people that you've been taught to respect, liars. Maybe not liars in the sense that they know they are perpetuating a falsehood, but liars in the sense that they haven't thought about whether they're telling you the truth—and in fact are telling you lies, which they probably believe themselves. These people very likely do love you and care about you, but that doesn't make the religion that they force upon you true, and it doesn't make the practice of indoctrinating children with nonsense acceptable.

Once your mind is free, you might even be angry with your parents or other guardians, but try not to be. In all likelihood they too were abused by religious indoctrination when they were young, or else they may not have the critical tools necessary to question authority, even when that authority says the most bizarre things. Whatever the case, please understand that there is no need to be disrespectful toward religious people; but you don't have to respect their beliefs.

This is not to say that all religions are equally harmful. I rather admire, for example, much of what the Quaker religion (a faith that focuses on works and a belief in equality rather than written dogma) has given to the world, even though I disagree with their position on god's existence. For the most part, this book will be slashing away at the notion of the Judeo-Christian-Islamic god. I realize that very few Muslims will have access to this book, so the focus here will mostly be on beliefs that are central to Christianity. Given this, I hope the reader will bear in mind that Islam (like Mormonism) is merely an add-on to the beliefs of the Christian religion and that all of the arguments against the existence of God also apply to Allah. If religion is a disease, then it makes sense to create a vaccine which will inoculate the largest number of people—so the emphasis here will be on Christianity.

However, even the kinder religions, those that meekly proclaim that they bring their followers a sense of peace, enlightenment, or community, promote habits of irrational thought that can lead to dangerous places or, at the very least, waste an awful lot of time.

No matter what your faith is, I'll undermine some of the ideas that you've been taught to believe in the most. I'll be taking away a lot: your comfort in prayer; the search for enlightenment; the image of a loving god; and the image of an afterlife. I'll have to tell you that, no, you won't get to see your grandparents again in heaven someday. No pet dogs or goldfish are waiting for you on some cloud in the sky. No one is listening to your prayers. If you hurt, it's not for a reason. God does not have a plan for you. He doesn't exist.

What I can offer you in place of all that is much better—because it's true.

1

The Invisible Flying Clown

We might as well begin by picking on the Judeo-Christian god. He's no more real than any of the other gods, but he does hold a more prominent place in the English-speaking world than those funny Eastern gods, some of whom have more than their share of arms!

All of the arguments for the existence of the Christian god are as absurd as the arguments for a Muslim god, Hindu gods, a Norse god, or Greek gods. The only thing these arguments have going for them is fear. The notion of an all-knowing, all-powerful god was forced into your mind when you were young, and the fear has stayed. Even people who aren't raised in a religious home can easily pick up the idea of a god, and a fear of him, from the culture. So let's not use the term "god": it conjures up fear when it should conjure up laughter. Below, you'll find a typical dialogue between a non-believer and a Christian, only we'll replace the word "god" with "Invisible Flying Clown." If you find the idea of an Invisible Flying Clown to be crazy, good. Rest assured that it is no crazier than the notion of a god. The evidence for the existence of both is exactly the same.

Believer: You should believe in the Invisible Flying Clown.

Nonbeliever: An Invisible Flying Clown?!

Believer: The Clown—IFC for short—is an all-powerful force for good. He created the entire universe out of nothing about 6,000 years ago and watches our every move, reads our every thought, and will one day judge us for our actions.

Nonbeliever: What does the IFC want?

Believer: He only asks that we believe in Him, and believe that part of Him came to the Earth as a human/god (we haven't quite worked this part out, so we call it a holy mystery), was born of a virgin, walked on water, healed the sick by touching them, was crucified, and came back from the dead three days later.

Nonbeliever: What will happen if I don't believe in the IFC?

Believer: Well, he will punish you.

Nonbeliever: Okay, I don't believe in him. Why isn't he punishing me?

Believer: Not now, stupid, after you're dead. If you don't believe in him, or accept that part of him came to earth as a half-human mystery man, walked on water, was executed, and all the rest, then you'll burn in a place called hell for all eternity.

Nonbeliever: What do I get for believing in the IFC?

Believer: Big rewards.

Nonbeliever: Like what? What rewards have you gotten so far?

Believer: Not now, stupid. I'll get them after I'm dead. I'll go to heaven and live with the IFC in eternal bliss, singing his praises and playing with the dog I had that died when I was a kid.

Nonbeliever: How do you know the IFC exists?

Believer: Well, the book he gave us tells us so.

Nonbeliever: What else is in this book?

Believer: Well, it tells the story of the IFC's chosen people, who started out in a garden with a talking snake. They both ate fruit from a tree they weren't supposed to eat from, and the IFC banished them from the garden and made it really painful for women to give birth. Then things went bad so the IFC destroyed the Earth with a flood, except for one guy, Noah, who built a really big boat and put two of all the animals in the world on it, including the dinosaurs, and floated around until the water drained away. One of his sons saw him naked, and Noah cursed him and his descendants to a life of slavery. Pretty soon the world was repopulated with people and animals and things got bad again. The IFC's chosen people were taken as slaves in Egypt, but they escaped because the IFC rained down plagues of frogs and bugs on the Egyptians, and then the chosen people ran away across the Red Sea.

Nonbeliever: They had boats?

Believer: No, the Invisible Flying Clown parted the water for them, and then later the IFC wrote down a bunch of rules for his followers on a stone tablet.

Nonbeliever: What was the first rule?

Believer: That you shouldn't believe in any other Invisible Flying Clown besides him. Do you want to hear the rest?

Nonbeliever: Uh, no.

Believer: Anyway, we know the Invisible Flying Clown exists because it says so in the book that says all that other stuff.

Nonbeliever: Well, for the sake of argument, let's say that I don't think that book is very accurate. Is there another reason why I should believe in the IFC?

Believer: Oh yes, look around you. The world is so complicated and complex that it must have required an Invisible Flying Clown to create it.

Nonbeliever: What created the Invisible Flying Clown, then?

Believer: Well, he created himself. He works in mysterious ways.

Nonbeliever: If you're going to say that the universe is too complex not to have been designed by a higher power, then why do you have to invoke something that must be even more complex to explain it? Isn't that contradictory?

Believer: I said that the Invisible Flying Clown works in mysterious ways. Besides, I know he exists because he answers prayers.

Nonbeliever: So, if I was sick and I prayed to the IFC, I would get better?

Believer: Sometimes.

Nonbeliever: Sometimes? Why not always?

Believer: Again—

Nonbeliever: Wait, let me guess. The IFC works in mysterious ways.

Believer: Mm-hmm. You've got it.

Nonbeliever: So, if I got cancer and prayed to the IFC He might help me and he might not?

Believer: Yes.

Nonbeliever: What if I lost an arm. Would he regrow the arm for me if I prayed hard enough?

Believer: Don't be silly.

Nonbeliever: How do you know the sick people he heals aren't getting better on their own?

Believer: Duh. If they got better on their own, then why are they praying? Let's move on. Do you know how the universe began?

Nonbeliever: No.

Believer: Does science have an answer?

Nonbeliever: Not yet, but they have several good ideas.

Believer: Well, then it must be the Invisible Flying Clown. Check and mate, sir!

Nonbeliever: InvisibleFlyingClowndamnit!

There are many more arguments, which we will deal with later, that we could put in the mouth of the IFC believer, but we'll break off here lest this become tedious. The tragedy is that I'm not dealing with the belief system of some fringe cult. I'm dealing with America's most dominant religious belief. Every single one of the absolutely crazy claims made by the believer in an Invisible Flying Clown is a central idea in Christianity. One need only substitute the word "god" for "IFC," and you've summed up the beliefs of a majority of Americans!

And to make matters worse, the nonbeliever above will not be defined as rational, but will be branded a "Nonbeliever in the Invisible Flying Clown," an "aclownist" if you will. I actually have to call myself an atheist! Why can't I just be thought of as sane?

We could put the IFC test to any religion and it would look equally as crazy as Christianity. Muslims believe that an Invisible Flying Clown sent an angel to a cave to talk to an illiterate merchant named Mohammed, whose only notable achievement up to that time had been to marry a rich woman, and that this man was the true prophet of the Clown, and that the Clown wants women to cover their heads and that people shouldn't eat pork. Jews believe that the Invisible Clown has not yet taken human form as a messiah and are still waiting for this to happen, and also believe that eating pork ticks the Clown off. All of them, Jews, Christians, and Muslims, believe that the Clown will one day come back and destroy everything in a fire of judgment and doom. And I didn't even mention that the Clown apparently allows a bad version of himself, an Invisible Flying Devil Clown, to wreak havoc everywhere as a lesson to everyone because our human ancestors in the Garden of Clowndom misbehaved.

Would any of this nonsense survive if it wasn't forced into you and others like you through clever indoctrination—through clever use of threats, fear, and flattery (being one of "the chosen")? It's not your fault that these beliefs have been stuffed down your throat. But you deserve better.

Let's begin the process of helping you reclaim your own mind.

2

Atheism as "Belief"

Perhaps the most disturbing passage in the Bible is in the book of Job. In this book, the devil challenges god to a bet. The devil claims that he can get one of god's most loyal followers, a wealthy and happy man named Job, to curse god if only god will let the devil torture the man. God accepts the bet and the devil promptly kills Job's livestock, his family, and then curses the man with sickness. Job is furious and angry even at the very friends who tell him not to give up belief. Eventually, Job cries out to god for an explanation. Surely, if Job is the creation of god (after all, Job, like the rest of us, never asked to be born), he deserves one. Job is a metaphor for humanity, and he is asking this question: why must we suffer, be tortured, and die if god loves us and has the power to stop all of this pain?

The Lord himself decided to answer Job. In her great book, *Doubt: A History*, Jennifer Michael Hecht quotes a few phrases from this biblical chapter. These are the words from the mouth of god. This is how god chose to explain himself, to explain the evil he either allows or causes:

Have you walked the depths of the ocean? Have the gates of death been opened to you? Where does light come from? And where darkness?

Hast thou entered into the treasures of the snow? Hast thou seen the treasures of the hail? Hath the rain a father? Who hath begotten the drops of dew?

Canst though bind the sweet influences of the Pleiades or loosen the bands of Orion?

Out of whose womb came the ice?

Who has put wisdom in the inward parts? Or who hath given understanding to the heart? Who can number the clouds in wisdom? Or who can stay the bottles of heaven, when the dust groweth into hardness, and the clods cleave fast together?

Wilt thou hunt the prey for the lion? Or fill the appetite of the young lions, when they crouch in their dens, and abide in the covert to lie in wait?

Gavest thou the goodly wings upon the peacocks?

Hast thou given the horse strength? Hast thou clothed his neck with thunder? Canst thou make him afraid as a grasshopper? The glory of his nostrils is terrible. (p. 68)

As Hecht points out, god's answer is simply to bury Job in mystery, to make him feel small and insignificant so that he will not ask such inconvenient questions in the future. God does not want Job to ask why he (god) would allow evil, why he would punish all the humans of the entire world for the sins of Adam and Eve, people that they had never even met. God does not want Job to ask what kind of teacher uses the suffering and death of children as lessons. In effect, god stares down upon the lowly Job and says: "You have no right to question me. Can you explain any of the mysteries of the universe?"

What happens when Job (humanity) lifts up his eyes and says to the sky tyrant, "Yes, I can"?

Aren't the answers to these questions the rock from the slingshot that buries itself in the forehead of the giant? The rock is science, and the sling from which it is flung is disbelief.

Ironically, the first step towards answering the mysteries that god put before Job is to stop believing in the very god from whose mouth the mysteries supposedly came.

* * *

Many religious people view atheism as simply another form of belief, no different from Christianity or Hinduism. It's not. It's the absence of belief. However, for a moment let's accept the assertion that atheism is a form of religion. (I don't really accept the idea that atheism is another type of faith, and I'll explain why in a moment. But for the sake of argument let's accept the assertion that atheism is just another "belief.")

Imagine if, of all the world's religions, one of them, say some little-known Christian church buried deep in Alabama, began to work miracles. Let's say that the members of this church, when they prayed and did their rituals, were actually able to heal the sick in high, statistically verifiable percentages. Let's say this church eradicated smallpox, and through its members' prayers sent people halfway across the world in hours, and to the moon in days. Let's say that its ministers were able to stare far out into the cosmos and down at the tiniest particles. There would seem to be nothing, given enough time, that these believers couldn't accomplish through their religion's rituals.

Wouldn't this little church win converts from all around the world? Wouldn't a religious sect with this kind of real-world power become completely dominant? It would be considered the one true faith. According to those who look at atheism as a belief, there is such a religion. It is called atheism, and it works precisely because it is so different from all of the other religions. Where the other religions assume that there are gods and a spirit world, atheism assumes there are not.

Let's define the "religion" of atheism in this way: "Atheism believes that questions of the natural world can be solved by beginning with the proposition that there is no god. Instead, the atheist looks at evidence before making a claim."

Okay, now let's assume that this "religion" of atheism has a ritual; it's called the scientific method. We've all learned it. One asks a question, sets up a hypothesis, runs an experiment, and then examines the evidence.

Atheism has now been defined as a "religion" with a core "theological" doctrine, and a "religious" ritual. We could stretch the metaphor to include labs as places of worship, etc., but it's unnecessary.

Let's now imagine our religion of atheism in the real world, where it must compete with other religions for followers. It's just one more piece of lettuce on the salad bar of religious belief.

The atheists, using their atheistic rituals, have conquered many of humankind's most destructive diseases. They have created artificial limbs, the telephone, flight, advances in agriculture and medicine. They have even managed to predict the weather. (Talk about prophecy!) They have created weapons technology capable of destroying the entire world many times over. Is this not a powerful religion? Has atheism not truly discovered the ways of god by simply assuming that there isn't one?

Imagine if any single religious sect could claim the kind of success in real-world results, for good or bad, that atheistic science has. Can you imagine if an evangelical

Christian church could pray a man into orbit? Would they hide this away and say that god works in mysterious ways, or would they scream it from the rooftops and win converts because of their supernatural miracle?

Atheistic science has been too successful. It makes the miraculous commonplace. If ever the world was destroyed nearly entirely, and some new race of intelligent beings, mired again in religious mumbo jumbo, discovered that we, the ancients, knew how to fly and how to prevent plagues, and could see hurricanes coming, wouldn't they think we had some powerful religion indeed? And if we could explain it all to this new race, wouldn't they be surprised to find that not a single one of our miracles was the result of prayer or religious ritual? That there wasn't a single word in any of our holy books about nuclear physics, about bacteria or viruses, about meteorology? We did the miraculous, we would have to say, by assuming that miracles don't exist and by ignoring the false teachings in our holy texts.

So if atheism is just another "belief," why doesn't atheism have a massive following? Why are atheists instead a small minority in America? Why are we reviled and pushed out of politics and public conversation?

It's because the advances of science are never described as being successful primarily because science assumes there is no god. Imagine a newspaper article that described a breakthrough in the creation of a smallpox vaccine:

> A group of atheists, working under the always successful assumption that there is no god and that the natural world operates without any supernatural help, found today that smallpox is in fact created by microscopic entities called viruses. Now that this evidence is in, the scientists can work on the creation of a vaccine using weakened viruses to strengthen the body's immune system. Another victory for the atheistic world view.

Don't you see? Everything that works in the world, everything that humanity has created works because we assume there is no god. Cars work because we assume that no god will help run them if there's no gasoline or engine. Diseases are cured because we assume that god has nothing to do with them; so scientists look for other causes. Buildings stand because we build them strongly, knowing that the hand of god won't hold them up.

Imagine building a car with no engine, and assuming it's going to run on "god power." What irony! After centuries of priests and shamans praying for signs and praying that a god or gods interfere with human lives, the only thing that has worked in the real world is to assume that god doesn't exist! To assume there is no god is to get off on the right foot every single time.

Let's imagine a situation where a child is badly injured. The child's deeply religious parents, assuming there is a god who works miracles, pray over the child in their home and do not take her to the hospital. The child dies. In this case, aren't the parents guilty of a crime? Don't we all, deep down, know that it's criminal to pretend there is a real god in certain situations? That injured child should have been taken to a hospital, where the doctors, who would assume that there is no god (through their actions if not their beliefs) would hopefully be able to repair her body and keep her alive. If there is a god, why does he demand that we deny him in order to make anything work?

Why don't we begin to define atheism as a religion? Not only that, but let's define everything that works as atheistic. Atheistic car mechanics, atheistic doctors, atheistic custodial workers. We could go on and on. Not a single profession in the entire world achieves results by assuming there is a god. That is, except for the religious profession, which exists only to perpetuate its religious beliefs.

But, you might say, don't many religious professionals do a lot to feed the hungry, clothe the poor, and all that? Don't religious people often do good things because of religion? Sure, but why do *they* have to do it? Because they know god won't. Religious people have to achieve real-world results in the same way that everyone else does: by assuming there is no god who'll do it for them.

If we did define atheism as a religion, then maybe we'd start to win converts in the same kind of numbers that Jesus and Mohammed have.

But we don't. Atheism is not a religion. What is it, then? It's an offshoot of scientific inquiry. Let me explain.

In the not-so-distant past, just a few centuries ago, people would look at the world and make guesses about how it worked. If a person was smart or well educated and wrote a guess down, then people began to believe it. Let's use an example you may have learned in your science classes: that of meat and maggots. It was once believed that if you left meat out in the open it turned into maggots. After all, that's what you saw if you left the meat out and came back a few days later. In fact, the idea that meat turns into maggots is just one of a seemingly infinite number of explanations for maggots.

Well, it's simple to test whether or not this is true. You put meat in two jars and put them both on a window sill. Cover one with a cloth and don't cover the other one. A few days later the uncovered jar will have maggots and the covered one won't. Interesting. Now you know that meat doesn't just turn into maggots. But you still don't know that maggots are fly larvae. It could be that the sun helps the meat turn into maggots. So try the experiment again with the jars in the shade. When the results are the same, you'll know that the sun is not a cause of maggots. But, if you're watching, you'll notice that flies are all over the meat in the uncovered jar. Could there be a connection? If you watch long enough, and closely enough, you'll see that, yes, the flies are laying eggs in the meat. The hatched larvae must live off the nutrition in the dead flesh.

By collecting evidence, you found the truth. And the truth is useful because you can build upon it. Once you discover, for example, that maggots eat only dead flesh, you'll find that they are excellent for cleaning the dead skin out of gangrenous wounds. This is an effective, though disgusting, medical procedure.

We reason in such a way. You begin by understanding something concrete and then building on it. Let's say that we don't know how sound works and that several of us are sitting around talking about the problem. One guy states that sound is caused by tiny little angels flying out of our mouths and entering the ears of the people we're speaking to. Any time there's a noise, it's the work of angels. If it's a really loud noise, then there are bunches of angels. The problem is that the angels get tired. If they have to fly too far, they give up or just fall down.

So this man creates a device that he thinks will carry the angels, and the sound, for long distances. It's a complicated machine, a large pipe with holes on the sides. Every five feet, the inventor has placed strong but silent fans. The fans are at the holes to give the angels a burst of wind to help carry them farther on.

Once the contraption is built, the man stations himself at one end of the pipe and puts another person at the opposite end a mile away. He speaks and the powerful fans start whirring.

Now, let's imagine that this inventor is in competition with a man who closely studied sound and discovered that it has a tendency to smash into an object, like a tree, but then seems to wash around the tree so that some of it comes around the other side. In fact, it acts rather like a wave.

This man realizes, because of previous scientific discoveries, that electricity, alternating current, is also a wave, and that it travels through wires. Well, if he wants to carry sound over long distances, it's not just a matter of turning the sound wave into an electrical wave, but changing it back into sound at the other end. So, he invents a device called a telephone that translates sound waves into electrical waves when you speak into it, and turns them back into sound waves when you listen to it.

Obviously, this is just a thought experiment. No one person could discover the nature of sound and invent the telephone. This is something that happens over generations, but it illustrates my point. If you start with a belief that has no evidence to back it up, then you'll get nowhere. The long-pipe/angel/fan machine obviously won't work, because there are no angels.

The telephone will work because there are sound and electrical waves. In the beginning, to say that angels carry sound or to say that sound is made of invisible waves may sound equally valid, or equally crazy, but one statement has the power of evidence to back it up and the other doesn't.

Likewise, if we begin with the idea that prayer really heals people, we will get nowhere. Prayer doesn't heal people. Prayer affects viruses, bacteria, and cancer cells about as much as ancient or tribal people dancing around a fire and killing animals for sacrifice does.

So, let's compare prayer with our example from above about the tiny sound-carrying angels. A contraption designed to convey sound-carrying angels over long distances doesn't work. Why? Simple: because there are no angels. Likewise, praying to god to heal someone doesn't work. Why? Simple: because there is no god.

The thing is, atheism is *not* a religion. Atheism is a simple statement of disbelief in any kind of supernatural force. This statement can be made with words such as "I don't believe in a god or group of gods." Or, it can be made with actions such as when someone goes to the hospital because he knows that god won't heal him. (And, I'm sorry, but the notion that god chose to heal a person through the creation of hospitals makes no sense. Where was god for the thousands of years that people got sick before hospitals existed?)

Once you've made that statement of disbelief, then you're free to think about every topic, be it moral or scientific, through the use of reason and your own intellect rather than by searching some holy book for the answers given by "prophets" of questionable sanity. Religions are an end. Atheism is a beginning.

Every religion claims that human beings are put on this Earth for the express purpose of discovering that religion. Atheism says no such thing. Atheistic scientific inquiry is merely a tool that anyone can use. It's like a hammer. And anyone can use a hammer. Scientific inquiry is like that. It doesn't require that you convert to any ideology in order to use it.

Even a deeply religious person can use the experimental method and have it work. To be an atheist merely means that you don't believe in anything, be it god, an Invisible Flying Clown, or sound-carrying angels, without evidence.

But wait! The religious person might be yelling at this point. You can't prove there is no god through scientific inquiry. He could easily exist and just chooses not to answer prayers. You can't prove that something doesn't exist! That's true. I can't prove that there aren't sound-carrying angels, either.

But, a liberal religious person might say, god does exist but he doesn't answer prayers or interact with the natural world at all. Then, I, as the skeptic, would have to ask: "How do you know he exists?" After all, the burden of proof is on the person making the claim. Prove to me he exists. If he doesn't answer prayers, if he doesn't interact with the natural world, then how do you know he's there? And, given the fact that he is either actively involved in the evil of the world or completely detached and uncaring, why do you think he is good?

The religious person will undoubtedly answer with the most harmful word ever concocted in the history of humankind:

Faith.

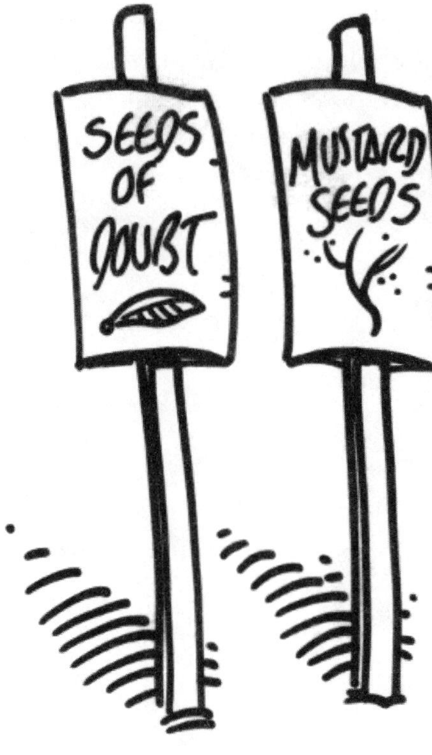
SEEDS OF DOUBT
MUSTARD SEEDS

3

Faith—A False Virtue

In our culture, perhaps no single word conjures up such positive overtones as the word faith. Religious people often proudly proclaim themselves to be "people of faith." Children are taught that faith is an important aspect of their upbringing. "We're raising our child in faith" is a common parental boast.

Faith is a central aspect of Christianity and Islam. But even religions that claim not to put a high premium on faith (that is, those that don't claim it's the golden ticket to heaven) still need faith. Religious Jews need to have faith that there is worth in carrying out the same rituals as people who lived and died thousands of years ago in a desert. They need to have faith that there really is a messiah on the way. Hindus must have faith in myriad (it doesn't hurt to look up a word now and then) gods and to have faith that good works will move them up the reincarnation chain to enlightenment. Buddhists have to have faith that the serene feeling that they get from meditation is somehow more spiritual than the feeling I get after going for a jog. In one way or another, faith, the ability to "believe," is an important aspect of all religions.

But why is "faith" held in such high regard. What does it mean anyway? The Oxford Dictionary defines faith like this:

1. complete trust or confidence 2. firm belief, especially without logical proof. 3. a system of religious belief; b. belief in religious doctrines.

Isn't this a strange set of definitions? First of all, faith implies a firm belief. The person of faith is usually a person who strongly believes in something. People of faith have little or no doubt about what they believe in.

Okay, you would think that people would have this kind of faith in things that have been proven to work, that is, things that have been proven true. I have unswerving faith that dawn will come tomorrow. It's come every day for billions of years! And I have faith that the gravity which has kept the Earth swirling around the sun will continue to work tomorrow and the next day and the next. Why? It's always worked. It's easy to have firm belief in something that is proven by evidence to be true.

And yet, the next part of the Oxford definition makes the first part seem bizarre. Faith is not just a firm belief; it's a firm belief, especially *without* logical proof.

Now wait a minute. How can anyone have a firm belief in something without proof for it? If I were to say that I had a firm belief in the existence of sound-carrying angels or an Invisible Flying Clown, people would think I was weird. If I said I had firm belief that the Invisible Flying Clown would rescue me if I jumped off a building, I'd be considered insane. After all, gravity is known to exist. One can have real faith in gravity. If something goes up, it comes down (unless it leaves the Earth's gravitational pull), but to put so much faith in something for which I have no evidence, to the point where I'd wager my life on it, would be nuts.

Let's revisit a slightly different version of an example I used earlier, but go into greater detail. Let's say there's a very religious farm family living out in the middle of nowhere, and the youngest boy has his leg mangled in a farming accident. The boy's mother and father, having been raised to have faith in the power of god, simply cover the boy's leg with a sheet and pray for him.

After one day of this, the boy is in extreme shock and delirium from pain and loss of blood. The mother calls her pastor, who contacts the other members of the church, and they gather to pray for the boy's healing. The boy gets worse and worse despite the prayers. One of the members of the congregation finally suggests that the mother and father take the boy to the hospital. They don't, thinking that if they show a lack of faith in god he will take the boy's life. The boy is only appearing to get sicker and sicker to test his and their faith.

The boy dies.

Any rational person, even a deeply religious one, would consider the actions of everyone involved, except for the injured boy, to be criminal. Why? Isn't faith a good thing, and the more faith the better? Why should having so much faith in god be a criminal and negligent act? Why should it be considered child endangerment?

Many religious people would answer that, while they believe in a god, they also believe that he wants them to visit a doctor. Most people see no contradiction in taking a loved one to the hospital and then praying to god for his or her recovery while that loved one gets all the help of modern medical science.

But if you really have faith, why go to the hospital?

In his wonderful book, *The God Delusion*, Richard Dawkins, wrote about a study called "The Great Prayer Experiment." It involved 1802 patients in six hospitals. All were recovering from the same type of heart surgery. The patients were divided into thirds. One group was prayed for and knew it; the second group was prayed for and did-n't know it; and the last group was not prayed for and did-n't know it.

It turns out that those in the two groups that were unaware of their prayer-status had no difference in their health or recovery. The only ones to show a difference were the people who were prayed for and knew it. They "suf-fered significantly more complications than those who did not [know they were being prayed for]." (p. 63) Dawkins attributes this to the added stress the knowledge brought.

This should have been an unnecessary study. A simple look at history shows that prayer does nothing. The infant mortality rate used to be much higher than it is now. Plagues used to ravage medieval Christian Europe and the Islamic nations of the Middle East. I presume that many people in these deeply religious societies prayed often and fervently and died horrible deaths regardless. Nobody in America dies of plague or smallpox anymore. Is it because we pray harder than our medieval predecessors? Or is it because science has given us better medicines?

Do we no longer have epidemics in this country be-cause god likes us better than people in the past, or is it because we discovered that sanitation and hand washing are effective in preventing outbreaks?

Ask yourself why it is that you're supposed to have just the right amount of faith. You're not supposed to have so much faith that you actually expect god to do anything useful, like heal the sick or rescue the helpless, but just enough so that you believe in very old texts and in wild stories. Believe just enough, the church seems to be saying, to get your behind in the seats every Saturday or Sunday.

Why do all religions put such a high premium on faith? Why do they ask their followers to "grow in faith," when clearly growing too much in faith can become a problem and can even land you in jail? What do the religions want? They want your faith to grow, but only in certain untestable areas. Religious Jews want you to have faith that a messiah is coming to save the world and that the books of the Old Testament are literally or figuratively true. They want you to have faith that Jesus was not a messiah, or savior. The Christians want you to have faith that Jesus was the son of god and that he was born of a virgin, walked on water, healed the sick, talked to Satan, was crucified for the sins of humanity, and that he died and came back three days later. The Muslims want you to have faith that Jesus was a prophet, but not the son of god, that god is named Allah, and that his true prophet was Mohammed, who was visited by an angel in a cave and spent his life conquering territory to spread Islam, taking many underage "wives" along the way.

How can these linked religions all exist? Simple: none of them have any evidence for their claims, so there's no way to test their validity. Each claim, without any real evidence to back it, is just as valid as the next. It is the absence of evidence, of logic, of reason, that forces all religions to put a high premium on faith. Because they have no evidence for their claims, they have to make it a virtue to believe in things that are illogical—even though in any other area to have faith in something without evidence is crazy.

Every single religion in the world teaches that you exist for only one reason: to find and believe in that religion, whatever it may be. They all teach that god went through all the trouble of creation just so you can have free will and discover his one true religion.

And most people believe that the one true religion is whichever one they grew up with.

How do the many churches of the world sell something as blatantly stupid, as sadistic, as faith? Well, they promise a lot, don't they? These religions claim that faith is the one thing that god requires. Many believers of various sects of Christianity and Islam think that god requires that we believe in him despite all evidence against his existence and the supposed truth of the scriptures. It is a virtue, for example, to believe in creationism and not evolution because of all the evidence stacked against creationism. The fact that there is not a single shred of real evidence in favor of creationism is only a test of faith. God wants to see if you will trust your own mind over the ancient holy texts he had written on his behalf. If you trust your own mind, if you lose faith that these comically flawed documents are the actual truth, then you will be punished. If you keep your faith, then you will be rewarded.

What are the rewards for having such faith, we might ask?

Heaven. A place of eternal bliss.

When do you go to heaven?

After you die!!

Of course, our next question is obvious: If you don't go to heaven until after you die, how does anyone know it exists? I think you know the answer:

You have to have FAITH!!!

And if you don't believe in all of this nonsense, what do the many religions of the world say awaits you?

Hell. A place of eternal torment.

Take a wild guess when you go. That's right: after you're dead. (You're getting good at this.) And how do we know that hell exists if people only go there after they're dead.

Drum roll, please . . .

You have to have FAITH!!!

Oddly enough, these extremes of reward and punishment, heaven on one hand and hell on the other, are enough to scare many people into being religious. Many people go to church and give money to it like they put money into a retirement account, hoping to do just enough to get into the nice gated community that is heaven and, perhaps more importantly, avoid that nasty slum called hell.

Isn't this insane? Isn't this a crazy wager? What if you picked the wrong religion? What if you're Catholic and god is a Southern Baptist? What if you're a Hindu and god is an African animist?

What if god wants you to conclude he's *not* there, and the only people who get into heaven are those wicked atheists? Why not? If you believe in a god who enjoys playing little games, how hard is it to believe in a god who tells everybody he wants them to believe in his holy books, but who really wants them to buck the system and *not* believe?

Of course, I don't believe any of this for a second. Many Christian and Muslim religious people are put off by the notion that people of other faiths, billions of people, are going to go to hell. And yet, if religious people want to believe that god lets people of all faiths into heaven, then what's the point of believing in any particular religion?

You see the problem? If you can get into heaven being a Buddhist, Muslim, Jain, or whatever, then why should you come to—and give money to—some Christian church? From the point of view of members of any particular religion, it makes no sense to say that everyone gets into heaven; and yet it seems cruel to condemn most of humanity to hellfire for believing, with total faith, in whatever holy book and religion happened to be fashionable in the area in which they were born.

This is a real problem for those seeking to sell religion, so they mostly ignore it. In America, it is a social convention not to argue about religion. We seem to have a policy of, "if you don't mess with my nonsense, I won't mess with yours." It's downright impolite to bring up the topic of logic to a religious person.

If you ever ask people who attend a "megachurch" why they give money to it, when it's plain for anyone to see that the tax-free cash is being used to build media empires and to line the pockets of already-wealthy preachers, they'll probably look at you funny. The truth is they don't care where the money goes. They give the money because they have faith that god is pleased with them for giving it, and is building them a nice retirement condo in the clouds.

Because religion is a business built on faith, it has to make faith into a virtue. Religions have to get to you when you are young and plow into your impressionable mind the idea that faith is a good thing, that it's the only thing that matters, that it's important. Not total faith, no, just enough faith to believe what god's spokesmen (and it is almost always men) are telling you, even when what they're telling you is complete rubbish.

Religions have to do this. After all, faith is their only product. Faith may consume your whole life and a good deal of your money and your intellect, but it costs religions next to nothing to produce it. And the best part? Every indoctrinated child grows up to sell the product to the next generation.

4

The Suicide King

(Arguments for God's Existence)

One of the more annoying aspects of talking to believers in god is that they always consider the god hypothesis to be the default position in any argument about the natural world. For example, a believer might ask you if you know how life could have "sprung up" in the first place. If you say science isn't sure yet, but has some pretty good, and testable hypotheses about how it might have happened, the religious person will seize on this. "But you're not sure, are you? Nobody was there!"

All of a sudden, people who will believe anything the Bible says on faith become the most careful skeptics when it comes to science. The implication of the above comment is that if there isn't any conclusive evidence on a topic involving the natural world, then "god must have done it." The religious seem to be saying, "If you can't prove it in front of my eyes, then my belief must be true." Or, if you can't absolutely show me how science explains this beyond a shadow of a doubt, then my religious ideas and your science must be on equal footing."

Nothing could be further from the truth. In fact, the claim that science is killing god is not true. God committed suicide a long time ago. The sharpest arguments put together to "prove" god's existence end up cutting god to pieces.

I'll go into the three most common arguments for the existence of a god, but before I get to them let me explain why they are so deadly to the very god idea they are designed to protect. Normally, when people argue endlessly about a topic it is because they are arguing from different beginnings or propositions. (As you've probably heard, there has to be some original point of agreement before two people can argue about anything.) For example, the argument over whether abortion should be legal or not will likely never go away because people cannot agree on the proposition. For someone who thinks that human life begins at conception, abortion at any stage is "murder." However, for people who think that human life begins at birth, then abortion is not murder. (The abortion debate is more complex than this, but the purpose here is to explain how arguments work.)

We are fortunate, then, that we have no such problem when dealing with the three most common arguments for god's existence. I disagree with all of their premises, but that won't be an issue because even when I pretend that I agree with them they obliterate the concept of a god. Here, then, are god's "suicide arguments."

God's Suicidal Arguments

1. The Prime Mover

It is a religious trick to dress absurdities up with solemn ceremonies in the hope that no one will notice their silliness. The taking of communion, for example, where Catholics eat a very sacred wafer that is supposed to change, at some point, into the flesh of Jesus is about as bizarre as you can get. Yet if everyone goes through the procedure with a solemn face, as if this is all very serious and important, then it appears to have some weight.

Sometimes atheists fall into the same trap and treat religious arguments with the same type of seriousness. So, any discussion about the Prime Mover argument generally begins with a long preamble about the deep philosophical thought of Aristotle, St. Thomas Aquinas, and blah, blah, blah. It's like putting a mule in a tuxedo.

Essentially, the Prime Mover argument makes the case that something had to cause the universe. That something, according to the religious believer, must be god. No effects exist without a cause, so there must have been some "first cause."

The reason this argument is so suicidal to god is that it brings up an even bigger question. Where did god come from? How does adding an all-powerful invisible entity at the beginning help us at all?

(In fact this argument is flawed scientifically. The universe did not need a first cause, and this will be explained shortly.)

Let's all just accept the Big Bang theory for a moment. The Catholic Church does, saying that it was the finger of god that sparked the creation of the universe. Well, we might then ask the scientific question of what existed before the Big Bang? We can have a lot of fun just throwing out theories without evidence. I could say that before the Big Bang all that existed were two wart-covered aliens playing video games. And one of the aliens got angry and threw his controller through the television set, thus providing the spark for the Big Bang. So, what we see now as "reality" is simply the video game running on, broken and partially haywire. You would laugh at this. Where did the aliens come from? Where did the television set and video game console come from? Sure, it's possible that this happened. After all, no one can prove conclusively that it didn't, but the absurdity of it makes this hypothesis seem unlikely.

And yet, people who would laugh at the Alien/Video Game Theory believe in the existence of a being who is infinitely more complex than they are, and who has created reasons for our existence which are quite bizarre. In fact, every "effect" we see in the universe has an easily explained cause. When I see a baseball flying through the air, I don't have to look very far to see what caused it—someone threw it or hit it. We could then ask a seemingly endless set of questions such as, "where did the thrower come from," etc., and we would have unremarkable answers all the way back until the Big Bang. Now, if we accepted god as the Prime Mover, he would be the only cause in this massive chain for which we have no explanation or hope of an explanation. This, somehow, makes him more likely to exist?

Science, as always, will simply say, "Well, we won't know until we can gather enough evidence to create a decent theory." Science does not insist upon anything that it can't prove. The idea of god being the first mover in the universe is silly and utterly without evidence. It should be of no more intellectual merit than the notion that a talking tractor, video game-playing aliens, invisible flying clowns, or angry raccoons created the universe. None of the arguments for a god are any better than the arguments for any of these things.

When talking about the origins of life, that is, when life actually began, religious people will often bring up a concept related to the Prime Mover argument. This is the principle of Occam's Razor, which is maybe the most misunderstood concept in philosophical history. (Even many professional philosophers miss what Occam's Razor implies.) According to the medieval philosopher William of Occam, if you are presented with two explanations for a phenomenon, then the explanation with the fewest assumptions is generally the right one. This is usually paraphrased as, "All else being equal, the simplest explanation is best."

To put this another way, Occam's Razor simply means that we have to consider the evidence without any "extras." We'll see what this means in a moment, and also why Occam's Razor is so dangerous to religion. (The medieval church, by the way, at least seemed to sense what Occam was up to and was not pleased—he died in exile. So, I'm not sure why religious people think his razor should be used on their behalf.)

When talking about the creation of the universe, religious folks will often invoke Occam's Razor and say: "What could be simpler than 'god did it'?"

Well, this is not such a simple explanation. First of all, we must make the mother of all assumptions—the existence of an all-powerful, invisible deity. Then we have to tack that notion on to any explanation we give for anything. So, God becomes a tumor that grows on the back of any explanation.

Let me show how Occam's Razor can be used to cut away the tumor from a more sophisticated argument made on god's behalf. The passage below is from a liberal and respected theologian who spoke up on behalf of evolutionary theory (and hence against the "intelligent design" proponents) at a trial in Dover, Pennsylvania. Catholic theologian John Haught was arguing that there was no conflict between science and religion, because, he believes, the two do not intersect:

Suppose a teapot is boiling on your stove, and someone comes into the room and says, "Explain to me why that's boiling." Well, one explanation would be it's boiling because the water molecules are moving around excitedly and the liquid state is being transformed into gas.

But at the same time you could just as easily have answered that question by saying, "It's boiling because my wife turned the gas on."

Or you could also answer the question by saying, "It's boiling because I want tea."

All three answers are right, but they don't conflict with each other because they're working on different levels. Science works at one level of investigation, religion at another . . . The problems occur when one assumes that there's only one level.

(quoted in *40 Days and 40 Nights*, by Matthew Chapman [Charles Darwin's great grandson], p. 106)

This line of reasoning made me think for a while, which is something that the god arguments have been inspiring people to do for years. However, it seems that Dr. Haught's argument cannot survive Occam's Razor. The idea that explanations can work on different levels is interesting. In fact, most actions do have several layers of explanation. The fallacy in this is in thinking that this includes a supernatural, rather than natural, explanation.

If I stated that the water was boiling because I wanted tea, then my want of tea could be easily explained through biological means. My body needs moisture and sends me signals to make sure that I get it. Ancestors that didn't have such signals would have died of thirst. Perhaps I was tired and my intellect, derived through evolution, would remind me that tea has caffeine.

If my wife turned on the stove for me, it may be because we have found that doing small favors for one another makes our marriage work better. Where, exactly, would I need god in any of these explanations? You see, if I was trying to observe and explain why water on a stove boils, the simplest explanation would be to say that heat causes the particles inside the water to move, that heat was caused by the electricity flowing through the heating element, and that the electricity came from a power plant, etc. If I believed in god, I would still have to explain the water particles, heat, etc., but I would have to tack on an extra layer of explanation at each point. Instead of saying, "The particles in the water are moving quickly because of the heat source," I would have to say, "The particles in the water are moving quickly because of the heat source and because an eternal, invisible deity of unlimited complexity designed this." Or, to use Occam's Razor to cut through Dr. Haught's several layers of explanation, I would have to say, "I want tea because I'm thirsty and because an eternal invisible deity of unlimited complexity wanted me to be." Adding a god, or an Invisible Flying Clown, or any other supernatural cause to an explanation makes it more complicated, not less. Occam's razor cuts no tumor more deeply than the one called god.

So, we see that the "prime mover" argument holds the seeds of its own destruction as does its companion, the misused Occam's Razor. If everything that exists must have a cause, and god exists, then where did he come from?

(By the way, if he's all powerful, could he make a rock so big that he couldn't lift it?)

2. The Watchmaker, er, Cell-Phone Maker

The second of god's suicidal arguments is roughly two hundred years old and was first put forth by the Anglican philosopher William Paley. The argument is rather simple. If something looks designed, then it must have a designer. A watch must have a watchmaker. In other words, if something is complex then it requires something more complex to create it. The universe, obviously, is very complex, therefore its creator must be, well, you get the picture.

Now, let's refer back to the believer's assertion that god as a prime mover, in keeping with Occam's principle, is a simple solution. As the great science writer/teacher/atheist Richard Dawkins has pointed out, any "Creator" must be at least as complex as his creations. It makes no sense to explain how something became complex by invoking an invisible, undetectable something that is infinitely more complex. In other words, if the universe is too complex to not have had a creator, then what does that say about the creator? If a watch needs a designer, then how could an incredibly complex creator just have sprung into existence?

In fact, the watchmaker argument, often used in conjunction with the human body, is not just suicidal but deeply flawed. For one thing, it ignores that many people are born with harmful birth defects that almost immediately cause suffering and death. Was the Watchmaker drunk? Secondly, the most complex things actually have teams of inventors, so it would seem that this argument actually is a better proof for the existence of many gods.

Thirdly, this argument is historically preposterous. Imagine a watch just popping into existence, fully formed. This is absurd. Everything that is complex in the universe has less complex origins. Modern cell phones contain cameras, video games, telephones, radio transmitters and receivers, and computers. The cell phone was not created before any of these other inventions, but was made up of them. And each of the cell phone's components had ancestors which were less complex. Digital cameras did not come out, indeed could not have come out, before Polaroids. Flat screen televisions with DVR capabilities did not come out before black and white television. The Grand Theft Auto video games did not come out before Pong. Nothing that is complex just pops into existence. The very nature of complexity is that it is made up of things that are less complex.

Further, if you grasp this, you would understand that the phones from the 1950s, the kind that Andy Griffith spoke into when he was calling Aunt Bee and Opie from the sheriff's office, could be considered a different species from the modern cell phone. Andy's phone did not want to become another type of phone. It did not consider itself to be a "transitional species" of phone, but merely survived for its time and then eventually found itself out-competed and then extinct. Only its fossil record survives in thrift stores, attics, and museums.

You might say, yes, the phone has evolved but it took humans (something more complex) to guide that evolution. Humans are a good metaphor in this case, but not for god, since no human being who grew up on an isolated island away from modern technology could ever hope to create a cell phone, or even conceive of what it is. (For that matter, imagine telling people fifty years ago that one day they would carry a phone in their pocket; I would bet that, almost universally, their first comment would be about how long the phone cord would have to be.) Human "inventors" aren't a good metaphor for god; but they are a good metaphor for natural selection. All that humans can do is look at all the phone designs that don't work (experiment) and then pick the ones that do. This is just a faster version of what nature does through environmental and sexual selection.

If I was ever brought into court to refute the watchmaker argument, I would find it an easy task. Every part of a watch had, at one time, uses that were entirely unrelated to its use in a watch in the same way that many of the features of a modern cell phone were once completely unrelated to being part of a cell phone. Numbers obviously had uses other than just being on a watch face. Gears were used for mills. The glass on the face of a watch was used for windows, and the strap is just a shrunken belt. When they all came together they turned out to have another use, at least partially unrelated to their original uses. Better yet, I could prove this. It would not be difficult to show the origins of numbers, of glass, of gears, of straps and to show that they had other uses prior to being part of a watch. I could even show "fossil" evidence of the antecedents of the modern watch. Egyptian sundials, Chinese water clocks, and the great designs which came from John Harrison's workshop (google his name; he's pretty cool) could all be used to prove the point that the watch evolved from smaller, less complex pieces. The evidence table would be full and the court reporter would have to stop and massage the tendons of her wrist when I was through.

And I could be confident that god would never show up to testify on his own behalf.

3. Why is there something rather than nothing?

The third of god's suicidal arguments is not really an argument. It actually involves an interesting question that theologians hope has an assumed answer. That is not to say the answer that believers give is interesting; it isn't. Religious people simply have to hope that believers will assume that the uninteresting answer is true.

We will now examine the biggest question of them all: Why is there something rather than nothing? Personally, I don't know why people assume there ever was nothing. What if the natural state of the universe is to be here? I don't know why people who live in a world of something should assume that there was at one point nothing.

Here's the problem with this question: Religious people don't believe there was ever really nothing, do they? According to them, god was hanging around, just waiting to create a universe so that he could make humans and play his little faith-or-hell game with us. This, then, is the problem. You cannot ask the question of why is there something rather than nothing if you don't assert that there actually was nothing. Instead, religious believers assert that rather than nothing, there was an Ultimate Something. This argument is the most persuasive when it is being used against the notion of a god. Why is there a god rather than nothing? Again, this argument is suicidal for the god idea.

It is here that we can also address the point I raised earlier about the universe not needing a "first cause" or "prime mover." Stephen Hawking (the really smart guy in a wheelchair who is often depicted in "The Simpsons") addressed the issue of the universe's creation from nothing to something and stated this in his best-selling *Brief History of Time*:

[T]he quantum theory of gravity has opened up a new possibility, in which there would be no boundary to space-time and so there would be no need to specify the behavior of the boundary . . . The universe would be completely self-contained and not affected by anything outside itself. It would be neither created nor destroyed. It would just BE. (p. 141)

Dr. Hawking is careful to point out that this is just a proposal based on the mechanics of quantum gravity and will remain a proposal until all the evidence is in. That being said, doesn't it make much more sense to theorize about the universe's "beginnings" (if the word even applies) from the standpoint of science than it does to theorize about it from the standpoint of religion? What, exactly, makes anyone think that a religious proposal is likely to be helpful here?

I prefer to address the question in this way. The question of "why is there something rather than nothing?" answers itself, since it is not possible to ask its opposite.

5

Evolution and Religion

Of course, we are, briefly, going to have to delve into the evolution vs. creationism issue. There is no issue among scientists—they almost universally accept evolution—and there are many other books by more talented writers that explain this better than I can. But if you're reading this, then it's likely that you've read some religious book at some point that seeks to demolish the "theory" of evolution. Religious authors try to poke holes in evolution in the hope that people will instead think "god did it." This is convenient for them, because creationists have not one shred of evidence for any of their claims.

Let's begin at the beginning. We won't waste too much time on this. We'll just put the heads of the religious anti-evolution pseudo-arguments on a chopping block and lop them off quickly, without much mess. We'll explain in the next chapter why fundamentalist religious people hate evolution (and why religious moderates should hate it). If you have ever been to a church or mosque or any other place of worship, then you've likely heard these assertions:

1) Evolution is a "belief." Religious people are so used to speaking in terms of "believing this" or "believing that" that they often don't understand that atheists don't believe things. We know things because there is evidence for them.

I'm often asked if I believe in evolution. What does that mean? It's like asking if I believe in gravity. If I don't believe in gravity, then what am I supposed to think, that angels are holding me to the ground?

In fact, "believing" in evolution is an easy thing to do. It just takes three steps:

1. Do you believe that two parents will create offspring with differing characteristics? (In other words, do you believe that children will be slightly different from their parents [and brothers and sisters] in height, hair color, and other attributes?) Of course you do. It would be silly not believe this.

2. Do you believe that these differences and mutations are caused by genes? There's no better-established fact in science. Genes are what make you you, and when a male and a female mix their genes, they produce offspring that are different from the parents and their other offspring.

3. Do you believe that in a natural environment some of these offspring will be better suited to survive and/or mate than others? (For example, do you believe that a gazelle that was born slightly faster than her mother or brothers or sisters would be more likely to escape a cheetah?) Isn't this obvious?

If you believe all of these things, then congratulations, you believe in evolution!!!

Evolution merely states that the offspring of two individuals will be different from each other and from their parents. This is universally true, except in the case of identical twins. In a natural environment, some offspring will have attributes that make them more likely to survive than the rest. If they survive long enough to reproduce and pass on their genes, the process continues.

2) Evolution violates the Second Law of Thermodynamics. The Second Law of Thermodynamics states that everything tends toward entropy. Entropy is a big scientific word for disorder. In order for something to be ordered, it requires energy. (By the way, the First Law of Thermodynamics is "Work creates heat." It has no place in this argument, but I thought you might be wondering.) It's easy to demonstrate the Second Law of Thermodynamics. Things do tend to become disordered if left alone. Don't clean your room for a month and it will become disordered. Don't mow your lawn for a couple of weeks in a rainy and sunny April and it will quickly become disordered.

It's embarrassingly easy to demolish this argument. First of all, it seems an odd argument to make from the perspective of a biologist. Not cleaning your room for a month would actually cause life to thrive in your room. You'd have fungus growing on pizza crusts, cockroaches finding love on your dirty socks, and so forth and so on. Biological organisms love places that are messy and disordered. The same is true in the case of an un-mown lawn. It's safe to say that if I never cut my grass there would be a lot more biological organisms in it than there are now. When I mow, my front yard becomes a biological wasteland. It seems that wherever human beings impose order, whether it be by using antiseptics or by building housing developments, it has a devastating effect on biological organisms.

And yet, animals are organized beings. Aren't we? We somehow get by. Doesn't this violate the Second Law of Thermodynamics? No. The Earth is an open system, not a closed one, and we get our energy from the sun. Plants soak it up and grow, animals eat the plants, and then they get eaten, and everything is recycled in a stunning variety of forms. If the sun ever went out, we would all die once

our independent energy sources ran out. Clearly, the evolution of life on Earth, pushed on by the power of the sun,
doesn't violate any law. It is curious, however, that creationists, who must know this, because scientists have been
pointing it out to them for decades, keep pushing the idea.
Maybe they hope that their audience won't check it out.

**3) Some attributes are too complex to have evolved by lit-
tle bits.** Things like the eye or a bird's wing don't work in
small pieces, therefore they couldn't have evolved slowly
and could only have been created all at once, or could only
have evolved with help from god. (The latter is the cornerstone of the bizarre "intelligent design" [ID] movement,
which is essentially creationism renamed).

We're going to spend some extra time on this, because
"irreducible complexity" is a fundamental idea in the cre-
ationist/intelligent design camp. Also, this is a very dangerous idea that has implications beyond science, so I want
to debunk it very carefully.

The cornerstone of this concept is the belief that evolution itself is too complex to have taken place without some
supernatural assistance. So, in a nutshell, an omnipotent
power chose to create human beings, but wanted to do so
slowly through evolutionary mechanisms. However, this
supernatural power found it necessary to jump in and tin-
ker with the process. ID proponents don't explain why an
omnipotent being would choose to behave in such a way,
why he would create an imperfect mechanism that would
require his intervention at key points.

But intelligent design is not a scientific theory, so questions like this don't bother its proponents. Intelligent
design is merely a criticism of evolution. ID proponents
claim that evolution cannot explain complex biological
organisms. For evolution to work, each part of a complex
organism would have to have been, at some point, a bene-

ficial mutation by itself. ID proponents claim this isn't possible, that a divine hand had to put the smaller parts together.

Creationists and ID proponents love to use the eye as an example of something that's "irreducibly complex." What they mean by this is that if you remove any one part of the interlocking parts of the eye, then eyesight as we know it would cease to exist, and therefore the eye couldn't have evolved slowly over time. According to the creationists, it had to have been created all at once. This argument has been debunked so many times that it's not even fun to do it again. So we won't.

Instead, we'll look at feathers. Creationists will sometimes point to a bird's wings and feathers as being irreducibly complex. After all, a bird with a few small feathers can't fly. What would be the advantage of having a partial wing, etc.? For evolution to work, wouldn't feathers have had to have a purpose at each stage of their development?

There's nothing at all wrong with this question. It's a very good one. The problem, as always, is in not attempting to answer the question and just saying instead, "god did it." The real answer is fascinating. There is strong evidence that modern birds evolved from dinosaurs. There are striking resemblances between, say, an ostrich and dinosaurs. For example, look at the feet of any bird and you'll see they are extremely reptilian.

Feathers did not originally evolve for the purpose of flight. Feathers, in the beginning, likely gave dinosaurs the advantage of being warm, or allowed them to put on displays. Feathers might have made a dinosaur "well dressed" and more likely to attract a mate, and therefore to pass on the gene for the creation of feathers.

Of course, if feathers attract mates, then the more feathers a dino had, the more likely it was to attract a mate. Those with the most feathers mated and then passed on the genes for more feathers. Etc. It was a bit like breeding horses or cows for size, only it happened naturally.

So, several generations of dinosaurs with feathers mated and created new generations of dinosaurs with added feathers until eventually one of them had so many feathers that he could glide for a short distance. If that ability gave him an evolutionary advantage, say the ability to see more prey from a greater height or to avoid predators, then he would be more likely to survive than his non-gliding relatives, and of course more likely to have babies that could glide. Those babies would glide farther than their father and their kids would glide farther than them, etc. This development wouldn't happen in a straight line—rather in fits and starts—but it would nonetheless head in the direction of flight.

You see, dinosaur feathers were originally used for warmth and to impress the opposite sex. However, it just so happens that the same things that were good for warmth and display turned out to allow flight. (New fossil evidence, of dinosaurs with pre-flight feathers, in support of this hypothesis shows up regularly.)

The odds against something like that happening are likely one in several million, but bear in mind that there are trillions of organisms in the world. And the Earth has been around for billions of years. The odds against hitting the lottery are high, but someone will hit it. (We'll explain this in more detail later with the rock star principle.)

Before we go any further, let's explore a specific way in which evolution works. Once we understand this, we'll be primed to go further into the argument. So, since this is a book aimed at young people, let's use one of my favorite fictional characters as an example. No, not Moses . . . Superman!

The Superman Principle

Unlike so many of today's fashionable superheroes, Superman was not a mutant. He was an alien. Superman's powers derived from his birth on the planet Krypton. There is an important biological lesson here. Superman, like all Kryptonians, evolved in an environment with a powerful gravitational pull. As a result, his muscles had tremendous strength. In the same way, if you were to go to the moon, your thigh muscles would give you tremendous jumping abilities. Why? Simple—you evolved on a planet with a higher gravitational pull.

Had Superman remained on Krypton, he would have been no different from anyone else on that planet. However, when he arrived in a new environment, he had superpowers.

The Superman Principle often works in exactly the same way when certain species are moved from one geographic area to another. If an animal has evolved in a certain way in its native land, then when moved to a new area, it may, like Superman, have the biological equivalent of superpowers.

For example, the brown tree snake evolved powerful predatory abilities in its native Australia and New Guinea. When it arrived in Guam, where the birds never had to evolve escape mechanisms from snakes, the brown tree snake treated the trees of Guam like a buffet. In just fifty years, the brown tree snake has wiped out nine of thirteen bird species on the island. (Most invasive species aren't so destructive, and there is much debate about whether new species are actually a bad thing or not—a case in point being the many parrot colonies in the U.S.).

Or, more dramatically, try to imagine what would happen if you took a cheetah—an animal that evolved to catch speedy gazelle on the savannas of Africa—and put her in a field of sheep. The cheetah would likely, for a while, have superpowers.

However, the cheetah's superpowers would last only for a time. Only a few generations would really be super. If Superman had a son with an Earth woman, the child would be considerably weaker. If cheetahs were fed on sheep for a few generations, then the species as a whole would slow down. Why? It's simple. Darwin explained it a long time ago. If you feed an animal, you take away the environmental pressures that shaped it. In the wild, only the fastest cheetahs get to eat, and therefore to mate and pass on their genes. If cheetahs were all feasting on sheep, then even the slowest cheetahs would get to eat, mate, and pass on their slow genes. Over time, the species would slow down. Superman can lose his powers.

All right, now if the Superman Principle makes sense, then we are primed to understand just how it was that the species you and I are a part of survived long enough to learn to read books.

Again, creationists/intelligent design advocates like to use the eye as an example of "irreducible complexity." Well, let's up the ante. Let's look at an ability that is much less common in nature than just being able to see. In fact, it's an ability that's so uncommon that it's unique to humans. It's an ability so complex that the human eye is just a part of it. It's the ability to throw accurately.

In his book, *Throwing Fire*, Alfred Crosby highlights research that shows that human beings are the only animals who can throw with precision. According to Crosby, the human ability to rotate our shoulders and throw things may have been the singular factor in the development of our large brains, and quite possibly could explain our rise to dominance over the larger animals. Crosby states:

> In order to throw a missile and hit a target the size of a rabbit at four meters, I must release the missile within a duration, "a launch window" of eleven milliseconds. That act, which most of us can perform some of the time and some of us all of the time, is in the same category of natural miracles as a bat's ability to snatch insects out of the dark guided by echolocation. (pp. 22–23)

I bet you didn't know that playing catch was such an impressive feat. Now, let's think about all of the "pieces" that are necessary in order for a human being to be able to play a game of catch. We need depth perception and effective sight. We need a rotator cuff. We need a thumb. If you remove any of these pieces, then the ability to throw accurately will be severely diminished. True, you can throw without a thumb and without depth perception, but to do it with split-second accuracy requires these things.

So how did humans develop this remarkable and complex ability? We didn't. All of the anatomical elements necessary to the ability to throw were developed in our tree-living ancestors, the small Australopithecine primates, who moved from the trees to the savannas of Africa five to eight million years ago.

Australopithecines likely developed very good eyesight while living among trees, where sight and depth perception (important for "tree traveling" as Crosby puts it) became more important than the sense of smell in the evolution of our human predecessors. (p. 18) Those primates with the best depth perception probably avoided running into tree trunks more often than those with inferior depth perception. This probably helped them not just to survive, but also, since females of all species tend to be less attracted to males who are always running into trees, to mate.

Eyesight was not the only gift that tree-life gave to our ancestors. Our rotator cuff, so important to later humans (especially baseball pitchers), also originally evolved among the trees. Crosby notes that the Australopithecines "had, like their ape relatives, upper limb structures (collarbones and ball-and-socket shoulders) that enabled them to revolve their arms in full circles . . ." (p. 19)

So tree-life developed in our ancestors both a sense of depth perception and the rotating shoulder, which likely evolved for branch-swinging, not for throwing. But tree-life wasn't done providing gifts to the Australopithecines. Our much-celebrated thumb likely also evolved there.

At the far, the distal, end of the Australopithecines' remarkable arms were the stunningly versatile primate hand, quite like our own, "the narrowest hinge" of which, according to Walt Whitman, "puts to scorn all machinery." The Australopithecine's thumb, nearly as opposable to the fingers and full palm as ours, was powerful yet dexterous, and was capable of instantly cooperating with the fingers in any number of kinds of grips, including, in all probability, the three-jawed chuck grip favored by baseball pitchers when throwing a fastball. (p. 19)

Once the Australopithecines moved from the trees to the ground, they likely discovered that they had been unwittingly equipped with the means for their own survival. Much later, as our ancestors became human, they carried with them these throwing attributes. This likely allowed humans to survive among, and later dominate, the more physically powerful large animals. According to Crosby, this was "a metamorphosis as wonderful as that of dinosaur feathers, probably evolved for warmth or display, becoming bird feathers for flight." (p. 21)

Okay, so now you see that all of the parts of our body that allow us to throw originally had different uses than what they came to have when they combined. Obviously, you need eyesight and depth perception to be able to throw. Nobody argues, however, that eyesight and depth perception aren't useful for reasons other than throwing. Their original uses were probably to prevent our little hairy ancestors from swinging into trees.

Likewise, the rotator cuff is necessary for throwing, but it's not just good for throwing, it's also good for swinging through trees. Our fingers and opposable thumbs are great for gripping baseballs and the like, but they aren't just good for that, are they? You're catching on.

God, Evolution & Disease

The eleventh chapter of Jared Diamond's brilliant book, *Guns, Germs, and Steel*, is entitled "Lethal Gift of Livestock," and he justifies that title with claims such as:

> The major killers of humanity throughout our recent history — smallpox, flu, tuberculosis, malaria, plague, measles, and cholera — are infectious diseases that evolved from diseases of animals . . . (pp. 196–7)

Diamond states that there are several animals that carry diseases of a kind that are very close to the types of diseases that infect humans. In a table titled "Deadly Gifts from Our Animal Friends," he shows that measles, tuberculosis, and smallpox all come from cattle. The flu comes from pigs and ducks. Pertussis comes from pigs and dogs, and falciparum malaria comes from birds.

Any human who lives closely with these animals is likely to get a disease from them. As well, as Diamond points out, animal domestication means a more settled lifestyle, one in which humans are more likely to come into contact with their own sewage as well as that of the animals they own. Diamond also writes:

> The importance of domesticated mammals rests on surprisingly few species of big terrestrial herbivores . . . Those Major Five of mammal domestication are the cow, sheep, goat, pig, and horse. (p. 159)

He goes on to include a chart that shows where these large animals come from. Sheep have a wild ancestor from West and Central Asia. Goats originated in West Asia. Cattle come from ancestors in Eurasia and Northern Africa. The pig descends from the wild boar which also comes from Eurasia and North Africa. (p. 160) So, since Europeans live with animals, they live with disease. If you understand how evolution works, then you can see where we're going with this. Hang on to that thought because I want to bring up one more thing.

The final piece of our puzzle concerns European beliefs about disease. In his book about the creation of the King James Bible, *God's Secretaries*, Adam Nicolson writes of the 1625 outbreak of plague in London:

> Disease exposes the assumptions of a society, and this ferocious outbreak of the plague throws the nature of Jacobean England into sudden highlight. People felt they understood the plague. It was a moral affliction which attacked cities because cities were wicked and disgusting. (pp. 23–24)

Likewise, Norman Cantor writes in his book, *In the Wake of the Plague*, about the Black Death of 1348–1349: "Inevitably, medieval physicians attributed the onset of the disease to God's punishment for sin." (p. 23)

The Europeans knew nothing of germs and believed that sickness and disease were expressions of the Wrath of God. This leads to a philosophical paradigm that looks something like this:

Truth: Disease is the Wrath of God.

Therefore: Anyone who gets sick from a plague must be wicked and deserves their sickness.

Therefore: If much of the city is sick, then the city must be wicked.

This is a classic example of "blame the victim" mentality. This line of reasoning was not applied in all cases, but it was the dominant explanation used by a populace that was baffled by the sudden onslaught of so much death.

And yet, amongst all the carnage caused by disease, something remarkable was happening to the European immune system. It was evolving rapidly and, unbeknownst to anyone, the Europeans were cultivating one of the most effective weapons of mass destruction in the history of the world.

North America was at one time populated by Native Americans, who had no large domesticated animals (except for perhaps the dog, which they usually ate). Europeans, in contrast, had pigs, sheep, goats, horses, and cows. And life with animals means life with diseases.

Europe became a breeding ground for all varieties of plagues and other diseases. Evolution worked its magic, and the people who survived the diseases had strong immune systems, were able to have children, and passed those strong immune systems on. Meanwhile, the Native American immune system was isolated from the viruses and bacteria to which the Europeans were constantly exposed.

Not only did Europeans have what Alfred Crosby called the "internal armor" of strong immune systems, but they had a world view that was light on science and heavy on religion.

The Native Americans, having lived outdoors and only having contact with animals on the hunt did not suffer from massive plagues, and as a consequence failed to buff up their immune systems. The question, then, is what is happened when the Europeans and the natives met?

The Europeans brought diseases for which the Native Americans had no immunity. Those diseases cut through the natives like a cheetah through sheep. And, since the Europeans knew nothing of germs, they brought with them the same beliefs about disease that they had in Europe. In other words, they believed that the Indians were being wiped out by the Wrath of God.

In fact, they were destroyed by smallpox, plague, and a variety of other diseases. It's likely that 90% of the American Indians on the East Coast succumbed to these diseases.

Let's look at a couple of quotes from James Loewen's *Lies My Teacher Told Me*. Check out this one from one of the great Pilgrim forefathers, William Bradford:

> A sorer disease cannot befall [the Indians], they fear it more than the plague. For usually they that have this disease have them in abundance, and for want of bedding and linen and other helps they fall into a lamentable condition as they lie on their hard mats, the pox breaking and mattering and running one into another, their skin cleaving by reason thereof to the mats they lie

on. When they turn them, a whole side will flay off at once as it were, and they will be all of a gore blood, most fearful to behold. And then being very sore, what with cold and distempers, they die like rotten sheep. (p. 80)

Like rotten sheep.

More importantly, let's look at this quote from a letter written by the Governor of the Massachusetts Bay colony, John Winthrop (also quoted by Loewen):

But for the natives in these parts, God hath so pursued them, as for 300 miles space the greatest part of them are swept away by the smallpox which still continues among them. So as God hath thereby cleared out title to this place . . . (p. 81)

Winthrop thought that the smallpox plague which destroyed the Indians was a gift from god. For Winthrop, the sight of all those non-Christians dying was a blessing. It meant that god was clearing the land for Christian use.

Of course, this is the same thing that intelligent design proponents would have to say if they acknowledged the logical implications of their "theory." If god shapes evolution with certain ends in mind, he must have known that the natives were not evolving immunities. And he must have known that the Europeans, suffering themselves through one plague after another, were building up powerful immune systems. In other words, god wanted a biological holocaust of the Indians. He wanted the white Christians to "have" America.

Now, either the ID proponents haven't thought about the wider implications of their "theory," or, what is infinitely worse, they have. Perhaps they want to see a design in the great biological disasters of history. Perhaps they, like Winthrop, want to believe that god really was clearing the American land for a takeover by white Christians. Let's hope the ID proponents are just ignorant and self-deluded, not evil. We'll give them the benefit of the doubt for now.

5. Evolution is a random process. To say that evolution could create a human being or an animal is like saying that a monkey banging away at a typewriter could create the works of Shakespeare.

(Sigh). Evolution is not a random process. The mutation process is random, but the fact that altered genes are responsible for the mutations is a fact, and, if a mutation gives an organism an advantage—either surviving in an environment or in attracting mates—then that mutation and the gene responsible for it will be passed on. And the offspring of the organism will have the mutation in varying degrees.

But, but, but, say the creationists, most mutations are bad for an organism, not good. This is true; the vast majority of mutations that occur in animals are bad. Those animals with maladaptive mutations usually die and don't pass on their genes. They aren't here for us to study. Only the animals who are born with useful mutations get to pass on their genes and the useful mutation, which means they are the only ones we can look at. (More on this in a later chapter.)

In his book, *Why do People Believe Weird Things*, Dr. Michael Shermer counters the "typing monkeys" metaphor. The creationists are actually off to a good start with this one, but they bungle it on purpose. A typing monkey is a good metaphor for mutations. The monkey obviously has no finished "design" in mind as he's banging away at the keys. What he hits is completely random. To expect a monkey to type the phrase "In the beginning," for example, would be too much. It would take a near eternity for this to happen if he had to type it all at once. But remember, evolution is cumulative. The mutations that are helpful are kept and passed on to the next generation. The metaphor would be complete if the monkey was banging away on a computer that kept the right letters (in a sequence that forms words) and discarded the rest.

If the computer was programmed to keep the "I" for example, then it's not hard to imagine the monkey whacking the "I" key randomly. It would likely happen very quickly. Then the computer would be looking for the monkey to hit the "n" key. When the monkey hit that key the computer would keep it and then move on to the "t" key and so on. All of the keys that the monkey hit that were wrong, or not useful in creating the phrase "In the beginning" would not show up and we'd never read anything but the finished product. The finished product—in this case, the phrase "In the beginning"—might look designed but that's only because we didn't see all of the hundreds of errant letters the monkey typed that ended up in the trash.

In nature, it's the same way. We don't often see bad mutations when we look at organisms. Those born with bad mutations end up in the metaphorical "trash can," and only the good mutations get kept in the sense that they get passed on to the next generation. Once a mutation is kept, the organism can move on to the next adaptation in the same way that our evolutionary typewriter keeps the letter "I" and then moves on to the letter "n."

(By the way, we'll move on to atheistic ethics later, but I should point out that no human being born with a harmful mutation should end up in any "trash can." We, as humans, have a duty to care for those who can't care for themselves. The natural world is a cruel place and should be no model for how we, as humans, structure our societies).

6. There are gaps in the fossil evidence for evolution. The fossil evidence gives no proof of one animal "turning into"another kind of animal.

(Sigh, again). ID proponents/creationists, tirelessly go on about gaps in the fossil evidence for evolution. They say there is no proof of a "missing link" between pre-human ancestors and humans. The truth of the matter is that there is an abundance of both paleontological and DNA evidence in favor of evolution. If there was not a single fossil on Earth, the other evidence for evolution would still make the theory indisputable. However, there are other greater problems with the creationist/ID claims. The very term "missing link" denotes a misunderstanding of evolutionary theory.

Let me explain by expanding on a metaphor that Richard Dawkins used in his book, *The Ancestor's Tale*. Let's say someone took two pictures of a man. The first picture was taken when the man was a newborn baby and the second picture was taken eighty years later when the man was very old. Now, if you showed these two pictures to an outsider unfamiliar with human development, say a space alien new to the planet—I know, that alien would be the product of evolution himself and would not be surprised by any of this, but bear with me—that alien would likely proclaim that he didn't believe that the baby and the old man were the same thing. The alien might incredulously ask you for a third picture, one that shows where the baby turned into the old man. This picture would be, from the alien's perspective, a missing link.

But you would know that no such missing link exists. In order to prove to the alien that the baby, in fact, gradually turned into an old man, you would have to show a steady progression of tens of thousands of photographs. If it was possible to take a picture of the person every day of his life from birth to old age, then you could lay those pictures out in front of the alien and show him a natural, steady progression of tiny changes that would lead from infancy to old age. There would not be a single picture among the tens of thousands that would definitively say that the man was an adolescent or an adult or an old man, not a single picture would allow the alien to say "Aha!" and point out the link between infancy and old age.

Evolution works in the exact same way. If each pre-human generation could have been fossilized, over millions of years, and the fossils laid out in front of us we would see a gradual and steady progression from pre-human to human with lots of dead ends and branches along the way. There would be no single fossil that would make us say, "Aha! There's the link," but we would eventually come to a time when there would be no doubt that the fossils, or bones, that we were looking at belonged to humans.

7. Since Evolution takes place over long periods of time, it's impossible to watch it happen in the lab; therefore we don't know if it takes place.

In certain circumstances, evolution can work rapidly, and scientists have watched it take place. A case in point is the evolution of antibiotic resistance in bacteria, which is easily observable in the laboratory and which has become a major public health problem.

Besides, the fossil evidence gives clear proof of the evolution of thousands of species, and besides that, all of the DNA evidence proves evolutionary theory. There's not been one shred of evidence found, ever, that contradicts evolutionary theory.

That being said, I'd love to see creationists recreate the stories in the book of Genesis in a lab. Whip up a man out of dirt and then grow a female from his rib, and I'll change my mind about evolution.

Conclusion

Intelligent design is actually worse than creationism because it makes the dishonest claim that it's a scientific theory. ID is a bizarre concept for many reasons. However the most bizarre thing about it is that it insults the creator it purports to add to evolutionary processes. Intelligent design states that a supernatural power must jump in and tweak evolutionary forces in order to make them work. The assumption here is that a perfect creator wasn't perfect enough to design a biological mechanism of change that didn't require him to jump in with a screwdriver and duct tape on occasion.

Most importantly, there is no way to test whether or not a creator is involved with evolutionary processes. ID proponents know this, and they know that the only way to try to gain adherents to their so-called theory is to try to poke holes in evolution, and then say that only god can patch those holes, without offering a shred of evidence to support that assertion. Thus, intelligent design is not testable. And, if it's not testable, it's not science.

When creationists actually make a scientific claim—as opposed to merely criticizing evolution and hoping you'll assume that the only other option is creationism—it doesn't pass the giggle test. For example, a new and massive creationist "museum" featuring dinosaur depictions recently opened in Petersburg, Kentucky. According to creationists, all of the animals that ever existed lived in the Garden of Eden, which originally had no predators, so all of the animals must have originally been plant eaters.

The problem here, of course, is explaining how a T-Rex, with its rows of razor sharp teeth, could have ever eaten plants. (Plant eaters evolve flat teeth for grinding plant material; omnivores, like us, that eat meat and plants have both sharp and flat teeth.)

No problem, according to the creationists: god originally made T-Rex with those great big teeth so that it could "crack coconuts." Once Adam and Eve "fell," the teeth were used for meat eating. T-Rex, I guess, died out in Noah's flood or sometime thereafter. Noah, by the way, supposedly carried baby dinosaurs with him on the ark in order to save room. I'm glad they clarified that. I was beginning to think that having dinosaurs on a giant boat was just plain silly.

Of course, the museum's curators lack any evidence for their claims. I guess they are hoping that their patrons will just have faith.

6

Two Columns: Science and Faith

Many believers seem to inherently understand that "faith" is a rather weak foundation upon which to build a philosophy. Faith isn't enough. Even the great Christian philosophers like Anselm, St. Augustine, and St. Thomas Aquinas were troubled by Christianity's reliance on faith, and tried to reconcile faith and reason. (This insecurity may be why religious believers often feel the need to obsessively gather in large groups. "How can I be crazy if everyone else thinks the same thing?" they seem to be asking.) As a result of this, many believers and some scientists (who may be trying to assuage public unease about science) claim that there is no contradiction between religion and science. They are separate rocks. Two great columns upon which the castle of human achievement stands. The two are, as the great biologist Stephen Jay Gould claimed, "non-overlapping." But as much as I admire Dr. Gould, he was wrong.

There are plenty of other people and institutions, like the Catholic Church (which accepts evolution), that also think that religion and science can coexist. Those who make this argument often have to engage in tortuous logic replete with contradictions. It is worth a detour to explore one of these glaring contradictions since it has such force in the world. Also, since it involves sex, it is rather interesting.

Most of the church's sexual laws (Catholic and Protestant) come not from the Bible, but from borrowed Greek philosophy. Aristotle's teleological argument makes the case that everything in the universe, whether animate (alive) or inanimate (uh, not alive, as you probably guessed) has a purpose ("telos" in Greek, which is why the title of this argument is such a mouthful). (Don't worry, we'll get to the part about sex in a minute.)

By this reasoning, everything in the universe is doing what it's supposed to be doing. Everything has a natural function and its actions define that function. For example, if a bird is building a nest, then nest building must be part of its natural function.

You may have noticed that this really isn't much of an argument. (A skeptic might claim, as scientists sometimes do, that it's so inane that "it's not even wrong.") This "argument" predicts nothing, but simply wraps itself around whatever is there. What something does is what it's supposed to do.

You might see the appeal for later Christians, who saw the world as created in one burst. Christians will simply take the phrase "everything does what it's supposed to do" and replace the word "supposed" with "created." Much of Catholic theology, particularly the part that deals with sexuality, is derived from the teleological argument. The thinking goes like this: Since sexual intercourse leads to pregnancy, the purpose of sexual intercourse must be to create children. According to the theologians, any other use of the sexual organs goes outside of what the sexual organs were intended for, and is therefore a perversion. This is why the Catholic Church opposed (and continues to oppose) forms of intercourse which do not lead to pregnancy—sex with birth control or homosexual sex, for example. This allows Catholics to oppose homosexual sex and yet stop short of calling for, as god did in Leviticus 20:13, the execution of homosexual men.

This argument is clearly flawed. Why do the male testes make trillions of sperm? Was each one created for the specific purpose of squiggling into an egg? Sexual impulses, as well as parental love for that matter, are clearly explained by evolutionary biology. Animals that like sex reproduce more. Animals that have to raise a baby, like humans, monkeys, and elephants, feel deep affection for their young; otherwise the youngster and the parents' genes would die out. Animals that do not have to care for their young, like snakes, most fish, or flies, show no parental attachment.

Evolutionary biology stands in contradiction to the teleological argument. Biology, and technology for that matter, is often driven by the fact that many things are used for other, usually more complicated things than what they were originally used for. (See the Watchmaker/Cell-Phone Maker discussion in Chapter 4.)

Somehow the Catholic Church embraces both Darwin and Aristotle, despite the fact that their ideas are clearly at odds with one another. The Church has not been pressed on this logical paradox, although it should be, since the Church's position on birth control and condoms has done untold harm in the world.

What this illustrates is the toxicity of the notion that religion and science can coexist in the same mind.

This also illustrates another important point. Liberal theologians and religious people who claim to embrace both science and religion may appear more rational than the creationists, but they aren't. The creationists at least understand that science and religion don't mix. What they don't understand, because they willfully don't want to, is that they are horribly wrong. If anyone says to you that religion and science can mix, force them to argue their case. They won't be able to counter these simple points: 1) Religion requires that you believe in something without evidence; 2) Science requires that you only "believe" something if there is evidence; 3) Usually, when religion makes a claim that can be tested, science finds evidence that runs counter to the religious claim.

Tell me again how science and religion can be brought together.

We have a fallacious tendency, due to our political system (and indoctrination in school and the mass media), to think that the middle ground is somehow always better. If there are those who say that god doesn't exist and there are fundamentalist religious folks, there is a tendency to see these two types as being at either end of a spectrum. In politics, people on either end of the spectrum are considered a little wacko by most of us, so some people think the same thing in regard to atheists and religious believers. The people in the middle must be the sane ones, right?

Uh, no. Let's apply this notion to a sun god. The sun sure looks like a god. It rises in the morning in a brilliant display and sets in the afternoon in the same way. It blinds you if you look at it. It brings life and can scorch the earth so that nothing will grow. And a whole lot of humans in early societies did worship it.

Let's say that we take three people. The first person is certain that the sun is a god. The second person is certain that the sun is just a big ball of gas that operates under purely material processes. The third person sees some middle ground, that the sun is partially a god and partially a big star. Who is right here? On what point should we agree, with all the evidence now in, with either the first or the third person? Whose idea would be correct? Whose idea would be the most useful for humankind? This is actually an argument that could have taken place just five hundred years ago if you were an Aztec. Science, as it took the mystery out of the sun, steadily encroached upon its godliness and then thoroughly destroyed the notion that it is supernatural. To put this another way, the third person mentioned above rested his belief that the sun is both a god and a ball of gas on the twin columns of faith and reason. And his belief fell because the first column could bear no weight.

In any event, there are two columns—but the kind we see on paper, not the kind that hold up castles. And it is possible to put all "beliefs" into them. You can simply draw two columns on a piece of paper and label one column "Faith" and the other "Science and Reason." Into these columns you'll fit two types of "beliefs," those that have evidence to back them up and those that don't. The beliefs that have evidence fall into the Science and Reason column and the beliefs that don't fall into the Faith column.

Leave lots of space for the Faith column, because the number of beliefs that can go into it is infinite. This disdain for evidence (as indicated by the mere existence of the ideas in the Faith column), and the accompanying willingness to believe almost anything, is why all religious belief, no matter how benign it might seem, is dangerous. For example, the Buddhist search for enlightenment or nirvana might seem harmless, but there is no evidence at all that there is any such thing as nirvana or that there is any way to reach harmony with the universe, whatever that means. (How does one reach harmony with space dust or Alpha Centauri?) Therefore, the Buddhist search for enlightenment falls into the faith category, where it coexists with all of the other faith-based beliefs, including those that claim that someone who commits a suicide bombing on behalf of Allah will go straight to heaven.

Religious people often cringe when atheists claim not to believe in anything not backed by evidence. This seems, to the religious, to be a very close-minded approach. How can you be an open-minded person when you refuse to think outside the column of scientific evidence? Well, what's the alternative? If there's no evidence for a belief, then it immediately falls into the "faith" column, where it resides with an infinite number of other beliefs for which there is no evidence. All religion does is pick out a select few beliefs from this infinitely large mosaic of unsupported beliefs and insist on their truth.

As I have painstakingly explained, all of the attempts to move the "god" belief from the Faith column into the Science and Reason column have failed. There is no scientific evidence for god; therefore, he lives in the same column as the Invisible Flying Clown, forest fairies, a fat man with a white beard and a chimney fetish, and shows on MTV worth watching.

And this is the problem with even the most harmless forms of religion. Even the most liberal Protestants who take their children to church are teaching them, by proxy, that wandering around in the faith column is perfectly acceptable. This teaches children to look at the many absurdities in the Faith column, even the very dangerous ones, and treat them with respect. After all, if mom, dad, and respected members of the community occasionally cross the line into this column, all of the ideas in it must deserve respect.

Even if religious belief doesn't act as a "gateway drug" to violent or dangerous ideas, and it usually doesn't, my other objection to spending time in the Faith column is simple: Why waste all that time and energy on useless religious thought? Isn't it a diversion? If you owned a computer which could aid in curing disease, understanding the universe, and creating great works of art, would you really want to waste any hard drive space and processing time by having it run programs on astrology?

How many minds have been ruined by religious ways of thinking? I know many intelligent young people from religious homes who could use their intellects to study math or science, but instead have to waste time memorizing the obscure laws of an ancient desert sect. Kids who could be reading literary classics all too often are handed the Left Behind series, which is nearly pornographic in its violence, and which exposes its readers to writing that is but a step or two above that found on the walls of public restrooms.

Also, there is the fact that, in a democracy, politicians must pander to the views of the majority. Certainly this is dangerous when the majority are taught to admire at least some concepts in the Faith column—where the ideas often came from the mouths of barely literate, post-stone-age desert dwellers—and to come to personal conclusions and voting decisions based on the answers made of air that they find there.

No. The ideas in the Faith column are equal only to each other, differing only in the amount of harm they do to human beings and to the ideas in the Science and Reason column that they so often try to displace.

The fact of the matter is that the second there is evidence for a claim or belief, then that claim moves into the Science and Reason column. If, tomorrow, scientists were to find compelling evidence for an Invisible Flying Clown, then that clown would cease to be in the Faith column and would move out of that bizarre neighborhood and into the Science and Reason column. The two columns, by their very nature, cannot overlap.

Still, some adults try to pretend that they can. What they really mean is that on occasion they like to put their reason into a little box and hide it away while they do a bit of slumming and take a trip from the Science and Reason column over to the Faith column. Why an adult would wish to pack away his or her rational thoughts and journey into Faith is beyond me, but I suppose that is his or her business. What I am opposed to is the notion that these adults have a right to take their children along for the ride.

This is not to say that religions should not be studied. They certainly should be. However, a trip to the Faith column should only be undertaken by an adult who has been solidly trained in the ways of reason. An adult trained to reason can wander through the museum halls of Faith without fear, studying the now-harmless skeletons of belief in the same way that I stare at a reconstruction of T-Rex, able to marvel at its once-fearsome power without fear of those jaws tearing my head off.

7

The Rock Star Principle

(Why Are We Here?)

Returning briefly to our earlier discussion of baseball pitchers and evolution, you may think it's a remarkable coincidence that we humans developed our ability to throw because our ancient ancestors lived in the trees several million years ago. You still might be tempted to believe in a god. After all, it seems strange that human beings are the only beings on the planet, and in the known universe, to have developed higher-order thinking, art, science, literature, architecture, etc.

But it's a mistake to look for any type of design here. Simply put, all of the animals that didn't evolve along with the environment were out-competed and driven to extinction; therefore, they aren't here to say how amazing it is that they are here. The same concept can be applied on a personal level. It really is amazing that I, the product of billions of years of random mutations and non-random natural selection, am able to sit here and type this. However, it's important to note that all of the other beings that didn't evolve through random mutations aren't here to type or to wonder aloud.

Why is it that when rock stars with hit CDs are interviewed, they always have the same story to tell? "My mom and dad and everybody said to put down that guitar and get a real job," the star usually says with an ironic smile. The rock star has made it, despite what everybody said to him. The moral of the story is never to listen to people who tell you to get a real job.

The thing is, nobody ever interviews all the wannabe rock stars who don't make it. Media types never interview some thirty-five-year-old guy living at home with his mom who says, "I wish I'd listened to my mom and got a real job." And yet, there are many more wannabes who don't make it than there are rock stars who do.

Why is this? It's pretty simple. Just about everybody with aspirations to be a rock star is going to hear the "get a real job" speech. The vast majority of our wannabe rock stars would be wise to take the advice, but there will always be some who don't, and a very few of those who don't take the advice do become rock stars. And becoming a rock star is a precondition to getting interviews and attention. All of the people who didn't become rock stars never get interviewed, and therefore you never hear what they have to say.

Isn't it odd, you might ask, that our planet is just far enough away from the sun that the sun's rays support life? We're not so far away as to be too cold and not so close as to burn up. In fact, everything around us, from air filled with oxygen, to food that grows in the ground, seems to be just perfectly tuned for our survival. How can this not be part of some divine plan? What are the odds against such perfect conditions?

In order to explain this, let's take a look at the iPod. In his book, *The Drunkard's Walk*, Leonard Mlodinow mentions the iPod Shuffle, which is designed to randomly play the stored songs in its memory. Well, the odds are that very occasionally, even if an iPod Shuffle was set up correctly and is working properly, one song might play six or seven times in a row. The odds against this happening are probably several million to one, but several million iPods were sold, so it had to happen somewhere, and probably would happen in varying degrees several times. In fact, Apple got a number of phone calls because people thought their iPods were not playing music randomly and were broken.

This illustrates two important points. One, there was nothing special about the people who had the iPods that played the same song six or seven times, in the same way that there is nothing special about a lottery winner. The odds say that someone will have an iPod that plays the same song repeatedly in exactly the same way that the odds say that someone will win the lottery. The odds just can't tell you who. That can only be done after the fact. The odds that any individual lottery player will win are exactly the same: purely random.

Secondly, when the improbable but inevitable did occur, and somebody's iPod played the same song repeatedly, the owner didn't assume that the iPod was infected with a demon or that a spell had been cast on it, but instead had the perfectly ordinary suspicion that something was wrong with the wiring or programming. The person with the "defective" iPod would probably have been a little p.o.ed if the good folks at Apple had told them that in order to get the Shuffle working again they should pray over it and maybe sacrifice a goat.

There's no reason to jump to supernatural conclusions about unlikely occurrences.

Now, let's up the ante a little. Everyone you meet, will meet, or ever have met is part of a far more exclusive group than our iPod owners or even our lottery winners. Everybody walking around is part of an incredibly exclusive club—what we might call the "sperm club." Out of all the trillions and trillions of sperm that your father created in his lifetime, you are one of the very few—or the only one—that fertilized an egg, survived the birth process, and became a human. Everyone around you is a member of that same exclusive club. Every human being that has ever lived is a winner of the longest-odds lottery you can imagine.

Yet, we consider it unremarkable that we are all winners of the universe's highest-odds lottery. Why? Because all the sperm who lost the lottery aren't here. You see, being the winner of this most improbable sperm/egg lottery is a precondition to picking up the winning ticket that is life.

Likewise, on planets where the conditions aren't suited to creating life, there are no life forms to look around and say, "Well, aren't we special?" Only on planets where the conditions are perfect for creating life do intelligent beings get to look around and say, "Hey, the conditions here are perfect for life!" If certain types of deep sea bacteria could talk they might find it remarkable that their environment, nearly devoid of oxygen, completely without sunlight, and hot enough to peel the paint off a Buick, is so perfect for them.

Also, think of this. Life capable of reasoning has only been on this planet for approximately 100,000 years, and over 90% percent of that time human society consisted of hunter-gatherer societies in which most of the intellectual energy was spent on simple survival. There could be plenty of planets out there that are fully capable of supporting life, and life that might even evolve into intelligent beings, but that are either in a stage that currently doesn't support life but will, or they have passed that stage. After all, to view the Earth four billion years ago would have been to see a volcanic planet with a poisonous atmosphere incapable of supporting life. To view Earth a billion years from now (or, regrettably, much sooner if we aren't careful),

might mean seeing a barren wasteland incapable of supporting life. So if we think we are special, then we need to realize that the odds against two planets entering an "intelligent life" stage at exactly the same time—let alone contacting each other—are incredibly long.

An even greater problem is the incredible distance between the stars. It takes about eight minutes for light to reach us from the sun. And the distance to stars is measured in light *years*. (The distance light travels in a year is about six trillion miles.) Care to guess how long it would take the fastest rocket ever launched to reach the nearest star (Alpha Centauri), which is only about 4.3 light years from Earth? 8 years? 81 years? 810 years? Try 81,000 years (according to the wonderful astronomy web site Universe Today—www.universetoday.com).

And we don't need to worry about hostile ETs seeing old episodes of "I Love Lucy" (or, worse, "American Idol") and rushing here to feast on us. Astronomers estimate that, using the biggest radio telescope on Earth, our old TV shows, radio broadcasts, etc. would only be detectable out to about one light year from the sun—only about a quarter of the way to the nearest star. This also means that using present technology it's highly unlikely that we'll detect radio transmissions from even the nearest stars, unless their inhabitants are deliberately trying to contact us with high-energy, highly directed transmissions.

Add to this that there are 200 to 400 billion stars in our galaxy, hundreds of millions of which might have life-bearing planets—at least they appear to have the potential—and it seems likely that the Milky Way is teeming with life. But, because of the extreme distances involved, we can't see or hear any of the other kids on the galactic block.

So, there is no reason for us to think that we, as human beings on Earth, are special in any way. The fact that we are the only known planet to have life doesn't mean that a higher power created us in his image (which seems kind of self-flattering when you think about it). It just means that life only exists in places where the conditions are right for it to exist.

Rock stars will only be interviewed if they make it. The only people who called in to complain about broken iPod Shuffles were the ones who, by random chance, had the same song play over and over. All of the people who don't make it as rock stars aren't interviewed. Only lottery winners get to collect the prize. And only on places where the conditions are right for life does anyone get to say how perfect the conditions for life are. Having the perfect conditions to create life is the invitation to the party of having life.

* * *

One of the more disgusting offshoots of religious thinking is what we'll call the Survivor Fallacy. This is where people who survive horrific events think there was something special about them that caused god to save them. Every day, for example, a certain percentage of people will be late to work. If you happened to be late on the day your

"LOOK! OUR WEDDING PHOTO MADE IT THROUGH WITHOUT A SCRATCH! WHAT A MIRACLE!"

office building collapsed, then there is no reason to think there is anything special about you. In fact, if you think there is, you are indirectly stating that god didn't consider those who died worthy of continued life and that you're somehow more deserving. Such humility. Even worse, if you think that god was trying to send you a message about your life through this disaster to others, then you evidently think that your epiphany was worth the death and mutilation of your coworkers and the suffering of their families.

This raises an interesting question. Why is god always communicating with humanity through earthquakes, disease, explosions, and suffering?

Hey god! We have e-mail now! You can stop sending your messages via dead children!

8

Does Anybody Ever Read This Thing?

(The Bible, That Is)

Let's imagine the following scene: A child comes home from school and she's very upset. Her mother is just pulling fresh chocolate chip cookies from the oven, but the child is so distraught that she won't touch them.

Mother: What's wrong, honey?

Daughter: My teacher read me this awful story in school today.

Mother: What was the story?

Daughter: It was about a father who lived in a wicked city and all of these ugly men surrounded his house and demanded that his male guests come out so that they could have sex with them. Instead, the man offered to let the men rape his virgin daughters. The town was destroyed and later the daughters got their father drunk and had sex with him, and then had his babies!

Mother: That's horrible! What book is this?

Daughter (sniffing and huffing): The, the, *Biiiiible*. (Breaks down in tears.)

This, of course, is the story of Lot and Sodom and Gomorrah from Genesis 19. It is the story of a man who offered to send his daughters out to an angry mob in order that they be raped, and who tried to entice the crowd by pointing out that his daughters were virgins. The girls were saved when angels blinded the mob of would-be rapists. One would think that, since the angels had this power, they might have said something to Lot about it before he went and offered up his children for brutal, forced sex. I am sure that the family dinner conversation was a little awkward that night. Lot was the only man in the wicked cities, by the way, that god chose as worthy to live. This was the man god considered to have high morals.

Can you imagine the reaction of parents, especially Christian parents, if an English teacher exposed their children to a non-religious book that had half the glorification of violence, murder, incest, rape, and destruction in the Bible?

It has become popular in atheist books to point out the many downright destructive and evil things that the Bible and the Koran command their religious readers to do. Religious people have no counter to this, other than to claim that the Bible or Koran must be read in their entirety. I don't know what that means. It's difficult to say that a command to, I don't know, slaughter people because they have sex with members of the same sex is taken out of context. Seems fairly straightforward to me.

I'll not spend an enormous amount of time laying out all of the terrible things the Bible sanctions. In his book, *Letter to a Christian Nation*, Sam Harris helpfully points out the many passages in the Bible that sanction slavery. Exodus 21:7–11 even allows a father to sell his daughter into sexual slavery! Likewise, in Harris' book, *The End of Faith*, he fills five pages with quotes from the Koran. All of these command the followers of Islam to kill or convert nonbelievers. These are religions of peace and love?

Instead of picking through the Bible and pointing out all of the commandments and laws that are morally disgusting, I'll simply pick two. These should be enough to show that the Bible is not just a poor guidebook to morality, but also that it deserves no attention at all when it comes to descriptions of history or the natural world.

In America, much has been made recently of the question of what sorts of rights homosexuals should have. Those who are opposed to homosexuals having the right to marry are also generally opposed to homosexuals having certain partner-related benefits such as insurance, death benefits, etc.

Why would anybody be against somebody else having basic rights? Moreover, how can the people who oppose giving others rights feel so righteous about it? How can they claim to have the moral high ground because they want to enshrine prejudice in the law?

The answer is simple: religion. Religion is the only force in the world that lets a person have his prejudice or hatred and feel good about it, too.

There is no logical reason to oppose allowing homosexuals to marry. Those who argue against homosexual marriage will sometimes say that the point of marriage is to have and raise children. Does this mean that a woman or man who is incapable of reproducing, or who has no interest in reproducing, should not be allowed to marry? Should we make heterosexual couples take fertility tests before marriage and sign a legal pledge to have children?

Some say that if marriage is opened up to homosexuals, then the institution will be destroyed and a man could marry an animal. Animal abuse and bestiality laws would obviously prevent this. This argument is a disgusting bit of propaganda, akin to the accusations made against Jews in Nazi Germany, where the Nazis attempted to make the love between two adults (a non-Jew and a Jew) seem like a repulsive act of bestiality.

Or, horror of horrors, allowing homosexuals to marry might allow a man to marry more than one woman or vice versa! What? I don't know how a law allowing two men or two women to marry would lead us on a course to polygamy. But if the religious folks in this country are hoping to make biblical or koranic law the law of the land, then they should support polygamy, because the Bible and the Koran both do—as long as it's the man who has multiple wives and not vice versa.

So, if opposition to homosexual marriage has no basis in logic or reason, then why are so many people in this country deeply offended by the idea that two grown people can fall in love with each other and marry?

The Bible is against homosexuality. God made Adam and Eve, say the religious, not Adam and Steve.

How clever!

But the fact of the matter is that all of god's followers are defying him at this very moment. Even by opposing gay marriage they are defying god. God doesn't want homosexuals denied rights. He wants them slaughtered, executed, killed.

Leviticus 20:13 plainly states this:

> If a man lies with a male as with a woman, both of them have committed an abomination; they shall be put to death; their blood is upon them.

This is supposedly a commandment from the mouth of god himself, as Leviticus 20:1 claims: "The Lord spoke to Moses, saying Say further to the people of Israel . . ."

If you believe in the Bible, then you must believe that not only did god say that for two men to have sex was a sin, but that homosexual men should be executed. (Apparently, god was okay with lesbians. Later, the apostle Paul was more inclusive and said that gay women should be killed, too. Talk about equality!) So if you're not actively hunting and killing gay men, then you are disobeying god.

Few religious people will (publicly) say that they support the execution of homosexuals; instead they say that homosexuality is a choice or a sin and that homosexuals can be "cured." But god doesn't want them cured, he wants them killed.

My question is this: How can Christians think that the first part of god's homosexual commandment is fine, that homosexuality is an abomination, but then back off on the second part, which calls for homosexual men to be slaughtered?

Either it's all true or none of it is. You can't accept the first part as god's will and ignore the second. If you are, then you are claiming that the Bible can be wrong on some things. Well, if it's wrong about homosexuals being murdered, then why isn't it wrong about homosexuality being an abomination?

Some Christians might argue that this section of Leviticus was meant to be the law merely for that small group of Jews that lived at the time of Moses and were under the direction of Moses. Fair enough. But let's remember that the Ten Commandments were also handed out by the same god to the same person, Moses, and then to the same people. If we throw out Leviticus 20:13, let's toss out the Ten Commandments as well.

There are countless passages in the Bible that call for vicious punishments for silly infractions. There are countless passages that sanction all kinds of morally disgusting things like polygamy, slavery, and the killing of nonbelievers. There's lots of stuff in the Bible that people ignore every day. Thank a nonexistent deity for that!

Likewise, we'll need to pick just one claim from the Bible to show that the book has no validity as a scientific document. All of the supposed "controversy" over whether or not Genesis is a scientific account and whether the Bible is an historical document can be wiped away, easily. While the Bible makes many false claims that science has laid waste to, many religious people simply refuse to accept scientific fact.

As I stated earlier, when creationists make arguments against evolution, they aren't actually trying to win a scientific debate. They are simply trying to give the appearance that there are two sides to the issue. Or they are hoping that religious followers will merely read the misleading creationist critiques of evolution. When the religious reader is satisfied that evolution is just a point of view or, worse, a false theory, then he or she will assume that creationism is the only other option. It's a ruse that's easy to put over on people who want to believe in creationism. The objective is to make the debate sound as technical and difficult as possible, so that the religious reader, or the layperson, will throw up their hands and assume that creationism and evolution are on equal terms, when nothing could be further from the truth.

Well, the Bible makes other claims that can easily be proved or disproved through experimentation. We'll take just one claim, again from Leviticus. Leviticus 20:21 says:

If a man takes his brother's wife, it is impurity; he has uncovered his brother's nakedness; they shall be childless.

Why is this phrase from the Bible so important? Simple: supposedly god spoke this phrase to Moses. It's a simple statement. God claims that if a man has sex with his sister-in-law, either while she is married to the man's brother or after, then the couple will be unable to have children.

Are there no cases in the world where a man has married his brother's widow and then had children with her? Are there no cases where a man has had sex with his brother's wife and gotten her pregnant? Are people serious when they think that the Bible is right about everything when a single episode of Jerry Springer could prove this statement to be complete nonsense?

Let's not brush by this. The Bible has made an objective statement that is either true or it isn't. This statement was supposedly spoken to Moses directly by god. This statement is verifiably false. If the Bible is wrong on even this one thing, why do some people assume it to be completely true and accurate on everything else? In fact, the Bible is rife with inconsistencies and nonsense, and Leviticus 20:21 is just one example.

Why do I hammer this point so hard? Darwin wrote in his book that if a single example of what creationists called "irreducible complexity" could be found, his theory would be nonsense. Creationists are always quoting this passage from *The Origin of Species*:

If it could be demonstrated that any complex organ existed, which could not possibly have been formed by numerous, successive, slight modifications, my theory would absolutely break down. (p. 219)

(Creationists tend not to quote the entire passage. Darwin's next sentence was "But I can find no such case.")

Creationists and "intelligent design" proponents, of course, drive themselves crazy trying to find just one example of an organ that is too complex to have been formed by numerous, successive, and slight modifications. They think that if they can find just one example then Darwin's theory would be finished.

Let's hold the Bible to the same standard. If the Bible makes just one claim that is verifiably false, then the "theory" that the Bible is the infallible word of god would be shattered. The Bible makes lots of false claims, and Leviticus 20:21 is just one glaring example.

Some religious people say that they don't think that every word in the Bible or the Koran or whatever is absolutely true. These people cherry pick through their religious texts looking for the parts that make them feel warm and fuzzy.

If you do that, then (at least subconsciously) you do what I do, and assume that all "sacred" texts are written by human authors who will sometimes have good ideas and sometimes have bad ideas. But you can't, for example, ignore Leviticus and treat the gospels of Mark, Luke, Matthew, and John as if they were absolutely true. Either they are the word of god and should be blindly followed or they are just documents to be examined. Either the books of the Bible are true or they aren't.

And they aren't.

But there are some good ideas in them, even if large passages are just made up. Jesus' parable in Matthew 20, where he describes a vineyard owner who paid the men who worked a full day for him the same as the men who worked a half day, and then told the men who complained,

"Friend, I am doing you no wrong; did you not agree with me for the usual daily wage? Take what belongs to you and go." This may have been intended to address the issue of late converts getting into the same heaven as lifelong believers, but it's a good piece of advice for other situations. Work for what you were promised and don't worry about what your coworkers are getting.

That being said, I have no illusions. Jesus wasn't born of a virgin, didn't walk on water, didn't rise from the dead, and didn't do anything else supernatural. These bits of biography were almost certainly borrowed from various earlier religions and mythologies. But if Jesus really existed and really said some of the things that are written in the New Testament, then most of his nonreligious ideas were good, if not original. He wasn't the first, for example, to command people to treat their neighbors as they would want to be treated. And he is very tiresome when he talks constantly about the kingdom of heaven, or when he implies, as he does, in John 15:6, that whoever doesn't believe in him and his sometimes egotistical rantings will burn in hell.

In fact, no less an intellect than Christopher Hitchens has pointed out, in his best-selling book, *God is Not Great: How Religion Poisons Everything*, that in some ways Jesus was far more vicious than the tyrant god of the Old Testament. Whereas god would command his followers to slaughter babies and destroy whole towns, he was at least content to have the torture and murder committed in his name confined to a short span of time. Jesus condemned nonbelievers, those who rejected him, to hell for eternity.

So, isn't he more of a condemner than a savior? If so, why is he so celebrated? Aren't those who slavishly follow him doing so primarily out of fear? As the Christian author C.S. Lewis has pointed out, if Jesus really did say what he supposedly said (and there's no way of knowing: the many gospels written about him were all written decades —or centuries—after his death by unknown authors, and many, perhaps most, of those written accounts were destroyed), then he was either crazy or the son of god.

If that's the case, then I have to make the same assumption about Jesus that I would make about anybody else who claimed to be the son of god: the man was crazy.

I agree with Thomas Jefferson, who produced a version of the New Testament ("The Jefferson Bible") in which he removed the miracles. All of the miraculous "son of god" nonsense took away from a pretty decent message about how to treat one's fellow human beings.

It's much worse for Islam. Take the "miracles" out of Islam, and you're left with a religion where the "true prophet" Mohammed thought nothing of slaughtering his fellow human beings in warfare and had no trouble treating women, even pre-pubescent girls, as sexual playthings and third-class citizens. And, oh yes, he approved the enslavement of non-Muslims by Muslims. He also condemned nonbelievers to hell, so Mohammed got to commit violence in this world and the next—and feel righteous about it. Or at least that's what the records of his life and teachings, written decades after his death, tell us.

9

Feelings as "Proof"

Some religious people, who are dismissive of science, think that the existence of god or a spirit world can be proved through the feelings they get when they pray. "God is love," they will say. "I have evidence for him because I can feel him." (I wonder what would happen if I said I "believed" in evolution because I could feel the power of the gene.)

This leads to an odd argument. "Prove to me you love your wife," a religious person might say to me, "show me evidence for love. You can't, because the evidence is not something that can be examined."

Sure it can. If I were to sit here and "love" a beautiful movie starlet, that would not be love, but infatuation. Sure, I'd have a feeling, but I'd have no evidence that I love her (and vice versa), and the fact that we've had no contact would confirm this. Love is defined through actions, as is heroism, as is cruelty. Actions define emotions.

I can't say, for example, that I love my wife and then, if she got cancer, walk out on her. Clearly, my action would be evidence that I didn't love her. I can't say that I love my son and then fail to take care of him. My wife and I show our love for our son every time we feed him, cuddle him, play with him, change him, or get up in the middle of the night with him.

Someone who acts kindly toward everyone can't be described as cruel. Cruelty is not a thing; it is a description of action. You can't be a hero without having done something heroic. To be a genius is to have produced a work of genius.

So I do have evidence that my wife loves me. If I didn't have evidence of it, if we didn't show each other love every day through action, then it would be silly for me to claim that we are in love.

Certainly I have an inner warm feeling for my wife and son, but I don't need to think that it's spiritual in order to enjoy it. Evolution explains these feelings easily. Individuals who have strong attachments to their mates and offspring are more likely to successfully raise children to the point where their children can reproduce, thus passing on the genes for strong attachments. Of course, relationships aren't that simple, and what kind of upbringing a child has plays a huge part in its development; but there is no reason for me to think that any of my emotions come from some spirit world.

I have no doubt that people feel something when they pray or when they go to church. It doesn't follow, however, that that feeling verifies the existence of some loving, all-powerful, invisible god that funnels people's souls into heaven or hell and reads billions of minds simultaneously. When people feel similar emotions at movies, sporting events, or rock concerts they don't attribute their emotions to a divine power. Praying may make you feel better if a loved one is sick, but so might taking a jog or a soak in a hot tub—and neither prove the existence of god or the devil.

So let's continue with this idea and stretch it a little beyond its starting point in this chapter. I hear over and over again that god is love—that he's a loving god.

What?!

Emotions and human characteristics are defined through actions. Einstein was a genius because he did genius-type things. Hitler was evil because he did evil things. Etc., etc. We define people by their actions or non-actions, and we should define our gods in the same way.

How can god or Allah be loving if he either A. actively causes horrible things to happen to people, or B. allows horrible things to happen.

This question actually predates the Christian-Islamic god. The Greek Epicurus famously put it like this:

> Is god willing to prevent evil, but not able? Then he is
>   impotent.
> Is he able, but not willing? Then he is malevolent.
> Is he both able and willing? Then whence cometh evil?
> Is he neither able nor willing? Then why call him god?

God should be defined through his actions, shouldn't he? Here we have a problem that religious people have never adequately resolved. If god is both good and all powerful, then why do bad things happen?

Religious people resort to all kinds of mental acrobatics to answer this question. *Evil is the absence of god,* some say. But how is that possible? God, being all-powerful, must have made a decision to remove himself and allow evil to happen. This brings up a real head-scratcher: How could an omnipresent god remove himself from anything? In other words, how could an omnipresent god not be omnipresent?

Evil is the creation of the devil. How does this absolve god? He created the devil, and he must have known what the devil would do.

Humanity lives in a fallen world. God created us in a perfect garden, and Adam and Eve chose to eat from "the tree of knowl-

edge"; and all humanity is paying for their sins. What in the hell is this? There was no Garden of Eden to begin with, and even if we accept the bizarre proposition that there was, then god must have known that Adam and Eve would eat the fruit from the tree of knowledge, which meant that he must have wanted them to fall so that he could punish humanity for all eternity. Talk about sick . . . And by the way, what kind of god would punish all women with painful childbirth because of Eve's supposed sin? Are women who accept pain-relieving drugs in a hospital making god mad because they are relieving some of the pain caused by the curse he put on Eve and all women in Genesis 3:16?

Let's accept, for a second, the insane idea that each individual human being is created by god. Then explain children who are born with birth defects so severe that they are unaware of their surroundings. Why does god create children with cleft palates and place them in cultures where he knows they will be shunned? Why does god allow children to be born into war zones where he must know they will be blown apart by bombs or land mines? Why does god allow some children to be born with their organs outside of their bodies so that what little life they have is spent in extreme pain?

For that matter, why doesn't god intervene when earthquakes bring the walls of buildings down onto children? Why do tornadoes crush people in the middle of the night? Why doesn't god step in on the occasions when a little girl is abducted, tortured, and murdered?

To the religious, there are only two answers to these questions. The first is "god works in mysterious ways." What this really means is that the religious person uttering this cliché has no good explanation and will not even attempt to provide one. The second answer is outright sick-

WANTED

For Crimes Against Humanity

ening: "god is testing our faith." This answer shows the self-centeredness of the religious person. Everything that happens in the world revolves around the believer and his or her faith. Everything is a test or a lesson from god. (As Nietzsche put it in *The Anti-Christ*: "'Salvation of the soul' —in plain words, 'the world revolves around *me*.'")

If this is true, if god allows evil in the world only to test people's faith, then the almighty is not a loving god but a sociopath. What is he doing, anyway? Is he sitting up in heaven allowing children to be killed, sold into prostitution, wither away from AIDS, or be gutted with machetes just to play some sick game? Is he saying, "Will you love me *now*? Will you still believe in me after *this*?" Or, "What if I let the devil do *this*? Will you still have faith in me?"

This is why prayer for a sick loved one, far from being a harmless act, is actually repulsive. Why grovel before the

very entity that is torturing (or standing idly by despite having the power to help) the person you care about? What does that say about the person doing the praying?

And, again, don't tell me that god's ways are mysterious and beyond our understanding. That's garbage and a non-argument. I wouldn't back out of a debate on evolution by saying that evolutionary theory works in mysterious ways.

If this is your god, then his actions or lack of action describe a petty tyrant, a sick bastard who shovels souls into bodies without regard for fairness, love, or happiness. He's a god who must enjoy all of the suffering in the world—otherwise it would not be here.

It's a good thing he doesn't exist.

* * *

Let's get back to the idea that fuzzy, warm feelings (when praying, etc.) are evidence for god's existence. The fact of the matter is that evolutionary theory easily explains emotions. Take the strong love that parents feel for their children. How can this be explained? Well, it's simple. In animals whose offspring have quite a bit of growing up to do outside of the mother's womb, like elephants, humans, apes, birds, and cats, there is always evidence of parental love. In animals where the offspring come out of the womb "ready to go," as in fish or snakes, the evidence of parental love is absent.

I watched a nature show a few years ago where a baboon grabbed hold of a baby gazelle and was planning to run off with the baby gazelle and eat her. Fortunately for the baby, the gazelle's mother was having none of it. She used her horns to ram the confused-looking baboon until he dropped the gazelle's baby and ran off. (It was hard not to root for the gazelle.

However, I learned the folly of this while watching another nature show where I was rooting for a group of sea lions as they swam through shark-infested waters. It was only a few minutes later that I realized by pulling for the sea lions to escape the Great Whites I was actually rooting against the penguins that the sea lions, having survived the sharks, so gleefully gobbled up. By rooting for the gazelle/mother I was actually rooting against the baboon's probably equally cuddly babies.)

Anyway, the mother's impulse to protect her offspring is at first surprising. Why would she risk herself to save her baby? Well, try to imagine what would have happened to the baby if the mother had no protective impulse. The baby gazelle would have been eaten, and the uncaring genes that his mother would have passed on to him would have been gone. In fact, the mother who loved her baby protected him, and those genes that caused her protective instincts survived (in the form of her baby).

The same is true in humans. Imagine what would have happen to a Stone Age infant if her parents didn't love her. Those parents would simply have her on the ground and their uncaring genes would have died with her. In fact, the genes for creating parental love had to have been present at every stage of pre-human and human development. Love, in fact, is observed among all of our monkey and ape cousins. No wonder the feeling is so powerful.

But it's not mysterious. Sometimes I actually hear religious believers say, "I can't explain my belief. It's like trying to tell your parents why you've fallen in love with someone who is all wrong for you. Logic doesn't apply." Sorry, but no; believing in god is not like falling in love with someone with whom you're mismatched. The person with whom you've fallen in love, flawed as he or she may be, actually exists. See what happens if you tell mom that you've fallen in love with the archangel Gabriel and that you plan to marry.

Please don't think that it degrades our emotions to explain them naturally. It doesn't. I love my son and wife fiercely, and that love is not in the least lessened because I realize the emotion has a biological and naturally explained basis. It is entirely possible, even likely, that parental love is the most powerful feeling in the universe and probably one of the most important things we would have in common with complex alien life forms (if we could contact them). That's a beautiful thing. As for me, I'm just glad to be here, and not to be a fish.

10

Let the Buyer Beware

The last stand of the religious believer is to try to turn the tables on the atheist. If skeptics insist on treating religious ideas like any other ideas, to be proven or disproven based on the available evidence, then some religious people figure that they can pull off the same trick. Why not treat atheism like any other religious faith?

If you feel sad as the logic of the anti-god arguments in this book seeps in, and slowly the realization that there is no heaven, no hell, no divine purpose to our lives—nor any particular reason to go through rituals in a mosque, synagogue, or temple—comes over you, that is natural. Your whole world view has just been shaken up. It's normal to be a little discombobulated. Don't let this feeling lead you into the illogical trap that is the Consumer Fallacy. This fallacy puts forth the notion that the customer is always right, and if the customer wants a comforting, omnipotent god, then, well, that's what the customer should get. It treats religious beliefs and atheism as if they were world views to be bought like boxes of cereal.

The "Atheism" box makes no crazy advertising claims, so why should anybody buy it? Why not go for the box that promises eternal bliss or peace, even if these are delusions? Religious advertisers make a key mistake when they put so many inflated boasts on the front of their box. Eventually, the buyer will get tired of just staring at the pretty ads and will want to tear open the package and see the goods they've been promised.

And when they do tear the box open, they'll find that it's empty.

An analogue of the Consumer Fallacy is the argument that religion makes people act better, and therefore it must be true. This is a bit like saying that the good behavior of children who believe in Santa Claus during the month of December proves the existence of a rotund oaf who thinks it's fun to lavish rich kids with toys while flying over homeless kids huddling on heating grates.

Some religious people will admit intellectual defeat once they realize that their arguments for religion are all rubbish. They might then say that they can't accept atheism because they can't accept a world without an afterlife or without moral absolutes. These people are admitting that they lie to themselves.

This form of the Consumer Fallacy is recognized by the way in which the religious make misleading claims about the atheist competition.

Consider this quote from David Berlinski's book *The Devil's Delusion*:

> What Hitler did not believe and what Stalin did not believe and what Mao did not believe and what the SS did not believe and what the Gestapo did not believe and what the NKVD did not believe and what the commissars, functionaries, swaggering executioners, Nazi doctors, Communist Party theoreticians, intellectuals, Brown Shirts, Black Shirts, gauleiters, and a thousand party hacks did not believe was that God was watching what they were doing.

First off, this is simply a form of the fallacious *ad hominem* attack (which means to attack the man rather than the argument; it's a common way to mislead people, and is normally used when those making the *ad hominem* attack realize that their argument is too weak to stand on its merits). Second, Berlinksi is strongly implying that the truth of ideas doesn't matter. All that matters is the results they supposedly produce. In other words, Berlinski is arguing that the ends justify the means. (The atheist position is the exact opposite: means determine ends. If you employ defective means [religion with all its lies and horrifying assertions], you'll produce defective ends.)

Third, some of Berlinski's assertions are flat out untrue. But, even if his statement was entirely accurate, Berlinski made a major mistake because his "logic" could be applied to literally every action, good or bad, ever taken by a human being in the history of the world. See what happens when I use his approach in a slightly different context:

> What Ben Franklin did not believe was that lightning was god's punishment for sin. What Edward Jenner did not believe was that smallpox was god's wrath. What Abraham Lincoln did not believe was that god sanctioned slavery, or that the Christian god existed at all. What the Russian and American soldiers who fought the Nazis did not believe was that god was going to stop the Nazi war machine. What aid workers in hospitals all over the world do not believe is that god is going to lift a single finger to help stop the suffering of children.

You see, Berlinski was attempting to make atheism look like a belief system, one that allowed for any crime to take place because there are no rules. Atheism is not a belief system. If atheists had a holy book it would be very small even if we used a very large font. It would contain a single sentence: "There is no god." At least it would be easy to memorize chapter and verse!

Religious believers indulging in the Consumer Fallacy try to make it sound as if atheists, because they don't believe that religion is the best way to gain moral footing, are therefore opposed to all forms of morality. Nothing could be further from the truth. Atheists have no anti-commandments. Again, we have one simple statement: "There is no god."

As I'll show, there are plenty of good reasons to act morally. Morality is a concept totally separate from religion.

Don't fall for the Consumer Fallacy. Don't let religion hijack your life and convince you that life has no meaning without a fictional heaven or hell or any other religious carrot or stick. You've been taught that meaning in life is something to be discovered. You've been taught that all humanity is here for one reason: to answer the question of what the meaning of life is. Each religion thinks it is the answer. (Note that I didn't say each religion thinks it *has* the answer. No, religions teach that they *are* the answer.) They give no logical positions but merely state that if you join them and let their dogma swallow you whole, you'll find salvation, revelations, or blessings. They are wrong.

Meaning is not to be found; it is to be created. You have a life and you have self-awareness. The fact that this grew naturally and without the help of any god or any spirit doesn't change the fact. All of the pain and pleasure in the world is without design, without purpose. The only entity that has the power to stop the pain is us, because we have no protector, no designer, no creator. We make both the good and the bad. Talk about responsibility.

You may ask the question: Is religion really so bad?

Yes, it is.

How much time and money are wasted in churches and mosques? How many people have been wracked with guilt over "sins" that harm no one? How many people have been taught that their own bodies are sinful, that women are lower than men? How much time and brain power have been wasted in senseless rituals and in the search for nirvana? It's sad that religion has poisoned so many lives. Think of the untold harm that simply one aspect of religion, belief in an afterlife, has done. Wouldn't we be less likely to send men and women to war if we knew that their deaths were an end and not a beginning?

You may still want to believe in a higher power, but why? I read an interview recently with a former U.S. president. The interviewer asked the former president what his image of god was. This is a revealing question. Why do people have to picture god? Doesn't that prove that he or she is just a figment of the imagination? If your image of god is an English grandfather and someone else views her as a six-armed female with brown skin, then what exactly are you all talking about, anyway? I mean, how does this work? Do you get to just make it up? Wasn't the reporter really asking the former president what his imaginary friend looks like?

You may also ask what happens after we die. Some atheists will even say, "Well, there's no way to know." I'll agree to that. I have no idea what happens after we die, but given the evidence, I'd say nothing.

The idea that my personality will live on after me is really bizarre. First of all, which me? I am not who I was when I was one year old. That version of my personality died a long time ago. If I die when I'm older and have grandchildren, then my grandchildren will picture me as an old man sitting on a cloud.

Here's why I don't "believe" in an afterlife. It's simple: my personality, or what is sometimes falsely called the soul, is dependent upon my brain being intact. If a certain part of my brain was injured or removed, say my frontal lobe, my personality would be drastically altered. Removing my frontal lobe would pretty much make me a vegetable. If removing pieces of my brain can alter my personality, alter me, then it's reasonable to assume that shutting down the brain would be the end of my personality. The end of me.

Am I sent into despair by this? No. I don't think about it much. I'm too busy living. Were you bothered by all the things that you missed that took place before your birth? If not, then why worry at all that you'll miss what happens after your death?

Being an atheist does not mean that you will become a stone-faced Mr. Spock. It doesn't mean you will not love and will instead go around judging everything as logical or illogical. It just means taking pleasure in what is really here. It means trying to make our society as good a place as possible. It means not deluding yourself.

Religion, in contrast, does irreparable harm to almost everything. For one thing, church organizations are parasitic. Churches add nothing to a community, but take tremendous amounts of money and time from their members. While it is true that many churches engage in charitable acts, it is also true that they do so only after they have paid the mortgage, the bills, and the salary of the preacher or preachers. It would be much more beneficial if people gave money directly to charitable organizations, without a lot of it being wasted on church overhead. (And let's not forget that churches pay no taxes, so the government services they receive, such as police and fire protection, are paid for by the rest of us—including nonbelievers.)

Some say that if there was no religion people would act immorally. If there's no god, they say, then there is no absolute morality, and if people don't fear god's judgment there's no reason not to sin and no reason to be good.

That's silly.

The argument that without belief in god there would be chaos, since there would be no divine judgment to fear, is not an argument for the existence of god. It's an argument that religion has a use, even if it is not true. In other words, the ends justify the means. And in this case the means are totally unnecessary.

A religious man might say that he doesn't murder people, do drugs, cheat on his wife, or beat his kids because god would punish him. If he really meant this, what it would say about him is frightening.

I don't murder people because I respect others and have empathy for them. I don't do drugs because they are harmful to me. I don't cheat on my wife because I love her and don't want to hurt our marriage. I don't beat my son because I love him and don't want to hurt him.

These are good enough reasons.

Along with the ends-justify-the-means assertion, religious people often like to drag out the tired argument that Stalin and Hitler were atheists, even though Hitler described himself as a Christian. This is silly. Atheists are freethinkers, which means we don't believe in dogma—including Communist dogma—and ideologies without strong evidence.

Religion teaches people to have faith. It seems likely that a society that has embraced religious nonsense for centuries is primed to believe in other forms of nonsense, such as Communism or Nazism. The Christian kingdoms of Europe, by the way, didn't treat the Jews much better than the Nazis did. So, it wasn't hard to turn the anti-semitic Christian masses into anti-semitic Nazi masses.

Fundamentalist Christians might be surprised to find how much they have in common with the "godless" Communists: 1) both look for their answers in revered books (The Bible / *Das Kapital, The Little Red Book*); 2) both worship saviors (J.C. / Lenin, Stalin, Mao, Castro, et al.); 3) both have exulted philosophers (Aquinas, Augustine / Marx, Lenin); 4) both believe in the physically impossible (transubstantiation / the "Dictatorship of the Proletariat" [the belief that rule by a small, self-appointed elite equals rule by the entire working class]); 5) both (supposedly) take their orders from abstractions (god / "the will of the people"); 6) both believe in the use of force (direct violence and institutionalized violence [government and its laws]) to impose their beliefs on others; and 7) both despise(d) the theory of evolution. (Stalin had evolutionary theory replaced with some nonsense called "Lysenkoism," which was basically relabeled Lamarckianism.) Warning: talking about this at parties probably won't get you many dates.

Still, I'll not argue against the fact that Stalin was an atheist and that many crimes were committed against religious people under Communism, at least partially in the name of atheism. Please understand, though, that this does not mean that atheists are evil. The horrible actions of Christian leaders throughout the world do not make all Christians evil, either.

As a student of history, I can say that whenever the government takes an official position on belief, whenever the government forces people to believe or give up belief, then atrocities are committed. I don't deny this. But again, the lesson is not that a political leader who is religious will always do harm, and it is not that a political leader who is an atheist will always do harm. The lesson is that political leaders shouldn't be forcing people to believe or not believe at all. I, and a vast majority of atheists, oppose any forcing of belief or non-belief on people.

Obviously, I am not advocating that the government make laws enforcing atheism. In fact, I am as repulsed by the way in which atheistic Communists treat religious believers in China as any good Christian is. I'm just advocating that the government stay out of the debate.

I know that if atheism challenges religion in the arena of ideas, then religion will be systematically dismantled, mind by mind. I know that religion, and the notion of god, survives only through the indoctrination of children, which is a kind of enforced belief in itself. My claim is simple: logic and reason lead one to atheism. Religious believers haven't learned to reason properly and, as a result, they want to deny young people the ability to reason properly. This is wrong.

And, as Sam Harris points out, no society has ever done anything horrible because its people have become too reasonable and inquiring.

There are those who think that god lies somewhere in human morality. Our moral reasoning is proof of god, according to these people. And there are those who worry that without an absolute law-giver humanity will have no clear direction and that we will fall into a watery form of what is called "cultural relativism," where all cultures, practices, and beliefs, no matter how abhorrent, are considered equal.

I'll answer both these arguments at once. Evolutionary theory explains morality just fine, and I can find morality with just my reason and genetically created emotions as my guide. I don't need a book. As a human being, I know how horrible it would be to lose a child or a spouse to war or natural disaster. I have mirror neurons in my brain that cause me to empathize with others, and so does almost everyone else. (Sociopaths may be an exception.) This is why people cry at movies, smile when babies laugh, and feel miserable when someone they know (or don't know, in many cases) undergoes tragedy. I understand the pain of others. In fact, the pain of others negatively affects me. I don't want to spread pain. Doing things that help others makes me feel better because I, and the people I am helping, come from the same genetic tree and share common emotions in the same way we share common senses like sight and smell.

Further, I dislike cultural relativism as much as any Bible-thumping minister. I am disgusted at the treatment of women in the Muslim world, horrified by the way that the lowest castes are oppressed under Hinduism, and repulsed by the behavior of the Communist authorities in China. I have no interest in relativism. I take a simple stance: Human freedom, up to the point where it interferes with someone else's freedom, is a good thing. Suffering is a bad thing. Anything that relieves suffering and spreads freedom is good. That which increases suffering and reduces freedom, especially freedom of thought, is bad.

If you're looking for meaning in your life, then assume there is no god and make your own meaning. That always works. As an atheist, I feel that there is much to do. I know, for example, that we humans are all that we have. No invisible being cares for us or is going to help us. We've got to do it. We've got to do everything for ourselves. If things are going to get better, it will be as a result of our actions.

Besides, there are times when I hold my young son or my wife and think that if this is all that there is in an otherwise empty universe, then that's enough. Go out and have as many moments like that as you can.

That's a box worth opening. That's a box with something in it.

11

The Darwinian God

At this point, you might even agree with everything written here and still believe in a god, but it will probably be what I call a Darwinian god. (This is ironic in that Darwin, with his long beard and deep-set eyes, looks a bit like the imaginary friend of many a believer.)

Those who believe in a Darwinian god believe that he set up reality so that all of the evidence points against his existence, and that he created human beings who could think logically so that their logic (fruit of the tree of knowledge) could be used to discredit his very being. According to this concept, the evidence against the existence of god is so intense because god wants to weed out those with the weakest faith. In other words, as science and reason increase the environmental selection pressures against faith, only the hardiest "species" of believers remain. And believers with this kind of absolutely irrational blind faith (sometimes called fanaticism) are the ones that god wants with him in heaven.

In some parts of the Islamic world, the belief in a Darwinian Allah takes a more practical form. Those who stray from the faith are executed, as if the very DNA of disbelief could be made extinct.

This is the most frightening and stupid form of faith of them all. Unfortunately, it's likely that as atheists become more vocal many moderate religious believers will concede that god does not exist, which is a good thing; but an intense and delusional group will remain and will likely become even more irrational.

There are already a good many religious believers who are so warped in their thinking that they do not care that logic and scientific evidence eradicate the idea of god. In fact, they think that their belief in spite of all the evidence is a virtue, and that as reason ascends "believers" are "under attack." They do not believe, really, that god is kind, because they relish the idea that their avenging god will brutally punish nonbelievers.

Believers in a Darwinian god shout that this deity is perfect not because they actually believe it, but because they believe god wants to hear it and because they want to be on his good side. They wail, cry, shout, and crawl on their knees to this vicious Darwinian god because they simply want to be on god's winning side. This is the form of Christianity popularized in the "Left Behind" novels about the violent rapture described in Revelation. The mega-bestselling status of those books is a frightening illustration of the popularity of this simultaneously vicious and groveling world view.

If you are reading this, and some version of the Darwinian god has been injected into your mind, please consider this an intervention. This Darwinian-god belief is a dangerous delusion.

Let's take this type of belief and put it in a different form. What if the same principles applied to a man who considered himself to be Napoleon? What if this man believed that he lived in the early 19th century? What if he believed that he was to be rewarded for his belief at some point in the future, perhaps during life or after death? According to his belief, any form of psychological therapy or exposure to reality would be simply a test of his faith in his belief. Which is more likely, that he is right or that he is deranged?

Even if you think he is deranged you may be tempted to think that, if the man is happy, that he should be left alone. It is even possible that, because he believes he is Napoleon, he acts bravely on occasion and you might observe that his delusion isn't all bad.

But think more deeply. What if he starts winning converts or, because people treat his delusion with respect, we see an outbreak of people believing that they are Abraham Lincoln or Martin Luther King, Jr. or Hitler? Or worse, what if other people claim to be Napoleon as well, and a fight breaks out over who is the real Napoleon? What if, some day, our Napoleon decides that it's time to recreate the Battle of Waterloo in a Starbucks with an AK-47?

Or, almost worse, what if he insists on teaching his children his toxic world view?

"FORGIVE ME FOR I HAVE SINNED. I DESTROYED ALMOST ALL LIFE IN A GIANT FLOOD, I'VE CAUSED PLAGUES, KILLED FIRSTBORNS, MADE CHILDBIRTH PAINFUL, MADE MY SON A SCAPEGOAT..."

12

Religious Indoctrination of Children Is Child Abuse

Ask yourself this: Why can't you raise your hand to ask a question during (or after) a Christian service? If you can't ask questions of a speaker, it must be because the speaker considers questions to be harmful or annoying. And if you are forced to be any place where questions are discouraged, you're likely being indoctrinated. Even in religious services, such as those that take place in many Jewish communities where questions are encouraged, there is at least one question that will probably get the questioner, especially if she is very young, in trouble. No, it's not "Does god exist?" The question is, "Can I go home?" (Prior to leaving the house, "Can't I just stay at home?" will do the trick, too.) Are children of any religious faith, before the age where they can inquire and think properly, really free to refuse to attend religious services? In the United States, the law is backward in this regard, giving no protection to a child's mind. Authority figures are not free to treat a child's body as they wish, but it is open season on the mind.

If a child's parents want to "shield" their child from the secular teachings of the public schools, if they want to teach their children dogma rather than science, that is considered the business of the parent. The law puts nonsensical belief above the welfare of the child. The child has no say in it. How is this fair?

To take advantage of the trusting nature of a child for the purpose of indoctrination is abuse. (Thanks to Richard Dawkins, again, for having the courage to point this out.)

You might think it's crazy to consider Sunday school to be abusive, but it is. In Sunday school, a nonsensical vision of the universe is hammered into your brain before you are old enough to intellectually defend yourself. This will haunt you for your whole life if you don't see through the nonsense. The people who are indoctrinating you are taking away your right to think critically. There is no greater theft.

What if I took a child and told her, every night and in every possible way, that if she ever jumped rope, invisible goblins in the sky would snatch her up and eat her flesh over and over and over again? Forever. If that child grew up believing this, living in fear of invisible goblins, and thinking that all of her rope-jumping friends were destined for a terrible fate, wouldn't you consider my actions to be horrible? Wouldn't it be abusive to take advantage of a child's trusting nature in such a way? This is exactly what religions do, threatening children with eternal torture for actions that harm no one.

So why do religions use such abusive indoctrination techniques? Religions are just like other businesses. The churches are selling something. Their product is universal: it is faith, and it costs next to nothing to produce, but it sells like hot cakes. Religions survive, because, like other businesses, they strive to form what corporations call "brand loyalty" in their customers. And churches, like businesses, try to hook their customers as young as possible.

All of the well known fast food establishments cater to children. They sell their garbage in a number of ways. The

DISBELIEF 101 • 125

idea is to get a child to think of the fast food as being fun, and to tie the food to a happy emotion. Kids get toys when they eat hamburgers that come in brightly colored boxes. If they eat in the restaurant portion of a fast food joint, there are places to play. The idea is to get them thinking about the food emotionally rather than logically. Emotions stay with you much longer than logical thoughts—especially when you're a kid. The fast food companies want kids to ignore the fact that they're eating junk, and instead focus on how happy they feel while doing it.

Places of worship do the same thing. Many churches use a double-pronged approach. They bring children in and try to make them feel good about going to church. Children are given comfort by the idea that they are loved by Jesus or Allah, that they are part of a select group (even if it's not stated outright, that they're better than everyone else), and that they will one day see dead loved ones again.

As a child gets older and is hooked, the church clamps down. The child is taught to be ashamed of his or her body, that sexual thoughts are sinful, and that there is a place of torment awaiting those who don't obey the church's restrictive sexual rules. So fear and self-loathing are added to the love, hope, and hubris mix.

Recently, many churches have resorted to flashier sales techniques utilizing Christian rock music and teen-oriented services. Legions of trendily dressed youth pastors with soul patches and earrings have descended upon teens, trying to assure them that Christ is cool.

The purpose of all this is not just to snare you, but to snare your children some day, and then your grandchildren.

Understand this: If religions don't indoctrinate children, they will cease to exist. They can only survive by using childhood indoctrination techniques. They bank on the fact that it's difficult to break free of indoctrinated ideas that were ingrained at an early age, especially for those who have been discouraged from thinking critically.

So what can you do? If you live in a religious household where saying you're an atheist will get you into serious trouble, then simply keep your nonbelief to yourself until you are old enough to do what you want. I am not advocating that you openly rebel against your parents or others in charge of you. They very likely love you and may be, on the whole, very good parents or very good authority figures. What I am telling you is that you and only you have the right to your own mind. It is illegal in this country to abuse the body of a child, but it's not illegal to abuse a child's mind. So you have to look out for yourself. No one else owns your mind. Only you.

What you can do, if you feel safe doing so, is to question authority. Ask your religious authority figures questions. Force them to explain their religious positions. When they do, keep in mind the Invisible Flying Clown test. Would what the priest is saying sound crazy if the word "god" was replaced with "IFC"?

Above all, realize that your mind, like your body, is your own. You don't have to let other people flood your mind with religious garbage. Religion relies and thrives on your fear. But don't be afraid. God doesn't exist. Say it with me. God doesn't exist.

He doesn't.

Bibliography

Cantor, Norman F. *In the Wake of the Plague: The Black Death and The World It Made*. New York: Perennial, 2001.

Chapman, Matthew. *40 Days and 40 Nights: Darwin, Intelligent Design, God, Oxycontin and Other Oddities on Trial in Pennsylvania*. New York: Collins, 2007.

Crosby, Alfred W. Throwing *Fire: Projectile Technology Throughout History*. Cambridge: Cambridge University Press, 2002.

Darwin, Charles. *The Origin of Species. London*: Penguin Books, 1985.

Dawkins, Richard. *The God Delusion*. Boston: Houghton-Mifflin Company. 2006.

Dawkins, Richard. *The Ancestor's Tale: A Pilgrimage to the Dawn of Evolution*. Boston: Houghton-Mifflin Company, 2004.

Diamond, Jared. *Guns, Germs, and Steel*. New York: W.W. Norton and Company, Inc., 1999.

God, Almighty. Holy Bible New Revised Standard Edition. Nashville: Thomas Nelson Publishers. 1989.

Gould, Stephen Jay. *Rocks of Ages: Science and Religion in the Fullness of Life*. New York: Ballantine Books, 1999.

Harris, Sam. *Letter to a Christian Nation*. New York: Alfred A. Knopf, 2006.

Harris, Sam. *The End of Faith: Religion, Terror, and the Future of Reason*. New York: W.W. Norton and Company Inc., 2004.

Hawking, Stephen. *A Brief History of Time*. New York: Bantam Books. 1996.

Hecht, Jennifer Michael. *Doubt: A History*. San Francisco: HarperCollins, 2003.

Hitchens, Christopher. *God Is Not Great: How Religion Poisons Everything*. New York: Twelve Books, Hachette Book Group, 2007.

Loewen, James W. *Lies My Teacher Told Me*. New York: Simon and Schuster, 1995.

Mlodinow, Leonard. *The Drunkard's Walk: How Randomness Rules Our Lives*. New York: Pantheon Books, 2008.

Nicholson, Adam. *God's Secretaries: The Making of the King James Bible*. New York: HarperCollins, 2003.

Shermer, Michael. *Why People Believe Weird Things: Pseudoscience, Superstition, and Other Confusions of Our Time*. New York: Owl Book Henry Holt and Co., 1997.

Stenger, Victor J. *God the Failed Hypothesis: How Science Shows that God Does Not Exist*. New York: Prometheus Books, 2008.

Index